Texas Whitewater

Texas
Whitewater

Steve Daniel

Texas A&M University Press
College Station

Library of Congress Cataloging-in-Publication Data

Daniel, Stephen H. (Stephen Hartley), 1950–
    Texas whitewater / Steve Daniel.
        p.   cm.
    Includes index.
    ISBN 0-89096-874-8 (cloth). — ISBN 0-89096-885-3 (paper)
    1. Rivers—Texas.   2. Drainage—Texas.   3. White-water canoeing.
I. Title
GB1225.T4D36   1999
797.1 ' 22 ' 09764—dc21   98–41877
                                                              CIP

Contents

Part One: Introduction

Part Two: Trinity River Drainage

Part Three: Brazos River Drainage

Part Four: **Colorado River Drainage**

Part Five: Guadalupe, San Antonio, and Nueces River Drainages

Part Six: Rio Grande Drainage

Illustrations

Preface

WHENEVER I PADDLE ELSEWHERE in the United States and mention to other boaters that I now live in Texas, I am always asked the same question: Is there any whitewater there? There is; otherwise, this would indeed be a very short book. But more often than not I am tempted to say "Not really," because to compare Texas whitewater to that of Colorado or the Southeast would only highlight the reasons serious whitewater boaters spend so much time traveling elsewhere.

Although Texas is blessed with all kinds of natural beauty, it has few dependable whitewater streams. The rare exceptions hardly compare to what one finds in West Virginia or California, making those of us who live here a bit envious. Most Texas boaters who want to improve their whitewater abilities beyond the intermediate level drive eighteen hours to places where bewildered locals shake their heads and wonder why we don't simply take up a sport we can pursue closer to home.

In Texas we annually look forward to hurricane season or winter storms that promise torrential rainfall. And when the rain does come, we try to make the best of it. Making the best of it is what this book is all about. It is about

Tonkawa Falls. Photo by Randy Barnes

beautiful scenery, long-lasting friendships, and challenges to one's physical and mental abilities. It is a summary of years of late-night drives, lengthy telephone calls, lost and broken equipment, and countless hours spent squinting over topographic maps. Because this book lists some streams that have yet to be run, it is also an invitation to another generation of whitewater boaters to continue the accumulation of reports, exaggerations, and anecdotes that make whitewater paddling exciting and mysterious to those outside the sport. It also provides some suggestions on how to discover other runs.

Chris Romine flies over Rio Vista Dam on the San Marcos River. Photo by Sheri Romine, courtesy Chris Romine

Because I am a whitewater kayaker, I describe Texas streams according to standards used in similar guidebooks for other parts of the country. This book is not meant for people who dabble in the sport or who worry about tipping over and getting soaked, but for boaters who have the equipment and experience to handle creeks that are runnable only when everything else is flooding. In other words, unless you typically wear a helmet and a life vest on the river, you would do well to stay off some of the runs described here.

Accordingly, anyone who paddles an aluminum or Coleman-type canoe or an inflatable raft from a discount chain, or who wears street clothes while paddling, would be better served by consulting the guidebooks to Texas rivers written by fishermen and leisure canoeists. Such boaters might consult sources such as *Texas Rivers and Rapids* (1972; 9th ed. 1999) by Ben Nolan and Bob Narramore; *An Analysis of Texas Waterways* (1974) by Harold Belisle and

Ron Josselet; and *A Guide to Texas Rivers and Streams* (1983) by Gene Kirkley. These books were written for the general public, before the development of most of the techniques and equipment found in whitewater paddling today. They provide prospective paddlers with information about where to go and what to expect, both on and off the river. Be aware, however, that the details provided about roads, access points, and rapids may no longer be accurate and that their exaggerated descriptions and ratings of streams would strike out-of-state boaters as amusing and outdated.

Instead of viewing whitewater as the limit of leisure paddling, whitewater *is* the heart of this book. That is why I include not only all of the whitewater runs described in other books but also many new (and to most boaters, unknown) streams. I focus on those stretches of rivers or creeks with the best prospects for whitewater. My recommendations about water levels and flows for these runs are based not on how much water is needed to float down a stream but rather on how much water is needed to create surfable waves, holes, and rapids.

In general, I avoid discussions of local attractions, camping facilities, fishing possibilities, and descriptions of how to run particular rapids. These topics may be of interest to some boaters, but they are not uppermost in the mind of someone who has just learned that three inches of rain fell in the headwaters of a creek that will be up and kicking for only a day or two. Of greater interest

Carol Taylor on a sit-on-top at Old Mill Rapid, San Marcos River. Courtesy Tony Plutino

is information on drainage areas, river gauges, and access points. For that paddler, I try to present a resource for making better decisions about where to go and for locating other runs yet undiscovered.

Of course, the lack of dependable whitewater is the reason paddlers in

Texas and elsewhere are unfamiliar with where the interesting runs are and how these streams compare with those out of state. To many who have spent their entire lives in Texas, the existence of some of these whitewater runs will come as a surprise. I have also tried to evaluate previously described creeks in a context that compares them less to one another than to whitewater in other states. Even someone from out of state can consult this book without having to worry that these descriptions have been compromised by the famous Lone Star penchant for hyperbole.

Boofing Borés (the Big One Relatively Speaking) on Austin's Bull Creek. Photo by Bruce Tate

For beginner and intermediate paddlers, this book is a useful resource on which they can draw as they improve their skills. However, since no other book on the market contains similar information, I suspect that it will benefit advanced boaters most.

I include information that will probably be obsolete in a surprisingly short time, such as how to access river data on the Internet. If the history of other books on Texas paddling is any indication, the road maps included in this book will become no more than general guides for getting to the river in years to come. Legislation and judicial decisions will undoubtedly modify some of the points about Texas law that Texas Assistant Attorney General Joe Riddell discusses in appendix C. Overall, though, I suspect that most of my descriptions are accurate enough to guide paddlers to streams that are among the best the state has to offer.

Acknowledgments

I WISH I COULD SAY that I have paddled every mile of every stretch of river described in this book, but I can't. It is not for lack of trying. Some of these streams are navigable only a few days a year, and when they are running so is everything else in the area. But other boaters have succumbed to their curiosity about local creeks that the rest of us never knew existed, and by pooling information we have a better sense of what is available.

Where I do not have firsthand experience with a run, I rely on reports from kayakers and canoeists with whom I have paddled and whose judgments and descriptions I trust. Even regarding stretches with which I am familiar, I depended on others for details about the stretches at various water levels.

In particular, I want to thank Bill Leon for his enthusiasm in exploring new runs in the Hill Country. If it weren't for Bill, many of the runs listed here might never have been made.

Bryan Craven and Todd Jackson contributed much of the information regarding runs in the Trinity River drainage. Don Daniel and Kendall Hemphill told me about some of the features of the Llano River, and Michael Van Winkle added greatly to my account of the South Llano River and the upper Guadalupe River. For my accounts of runs in the Bosque drainage near Waco, I turned to Joey Harrell. Charles McDonald and Robert McArthur filled in

Bill Leon on the upper Guadalupe River. Photo by Patsy Kott

Bryan Craven slides down the first drop of Pedernales Falls in flood. Photo by Rick Penney, courtesy Bryan Craven

gaps on the Lampasas River, as did Mike Smith on Rocky Creek, Mike Oehrtman on Bull Creek, and Jean McArthur on Shoal Creek.

Several raft guides gave me information about Terlingua Creek and the Hoodoos section of the Rio Grande. And any serious student of river running on the Pecos River and the Lower Canyons of the Rio Grande has to acknowledge a debt to Louis Aulbach.

Of course, I could have misunderstood things I learned, so I alone am responsible for any inaccuracies in this book.

This book's appeal has been enhanced substantially by photos from David Abel, Bryan Craven, Judd Cherry, Carolyn Allbritton, Chris Romine, Tony Plutino, Bill Leon, Steve Mills, Randy Barnes, and Michael Van Winkle. Neil Harrison contributed information on how to check river flows and weather on the Internet. Peter Newman resolved critical computer printing issues.

Some of the boaters already listed indulged my curiosity about unfamiliar runs by checking out streams that occasionally turned out to be less than we had hoped. Randy Barnes, Steve Mills, Jean McArthur, Jimmy Vick, Bruce Tate, Tony Cooper, Bruce Walker, James Holmes, Carolyn Allbritton, Thelma Coles, Mike Smith, and others have at one time or another been the ones I could find on short notice willing to paddle with me. I have learned as much about friendship from them as I have about the rivers we ran.

Though not a whitewater boater herself, my wife Breaux knows from years of being married to one how wet gear, nonstop paddling talk, carnage videos with awful music, and sleeping on the floor in strangers' homes are parts of a life that even those of us who live it dare not think much about. She has endured with grace and patience the long-distance phone bills, the worry-filled nights, and the uncertainty of not knowing whether Saturday's plans with her will be spoiled by a thunderstorm 150 miles away on Friday night.

One time Breaux spent Memorial Day weekend driving around the state with me to check on river access points, even going so far as to sleep cramped in the car when all the motel rooms in Junction were booked on graduation night. As if this wasn't enough, she also trained her critical eye on my text.

It is no overstatement to say that without Breaux's support I could not pursue my passion for paddling whitewater. In fact, I wonder if I would want to. It is to her that this book is dedicated.

Breaux before her only encounter with whitewater, Ocoee River, Tennessee, 1981

PART ONE

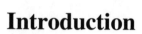

Introduction

Ben Kvanli surfs the wave at Longhorn Dam on the Colorado River in Austin. © David Abel

Overview of Texas Whitewater Streams

ALTHOUGH THERE ARE MOUNTAINS in West Texas, there is not much rainfall and no snowmelt runoff. After big thunderstorms some of the arroyos and draws in the Panhandle, the Davis Mountains, and the Big Bend region become churning brown maelstroms for a few days a year. Where the Rio Grande cuts through the mountains of the Big Bend, there is some whitewater but rapids are few and far between. In the southern and eastern parts of the state, the land is flat or characterized by rolling hills. River bottoms consist of sand, mud, or clay and seldom have the rock features that create whitewater conditions.

Between the mountains of West Texas and the piney lowlands of East Texas is a part of the Great Plains known in the Panhandle as the Llano Estacado, the staked plain. Southeast of Lubbock these high plains end at the Caprock Escarpment, where the land drops onto the 200-mile-wide low plains of

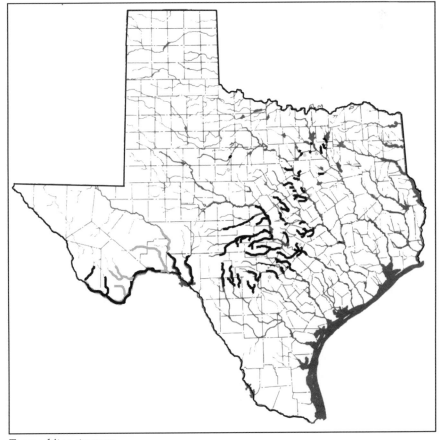

Texas whitewater runs

north-central Texas. To the south the high plains slope down to the limestone uplands (the Hill Country) of the Edwards Plateau west of Austin and San Antonio. The Edwards Plateau meets the Gulf Coastal Plain along the Balcones Escarpment, which runs roughly east from Del Rio toward San Antonio along US 90 and then north to Austin. Although the escarpment gradually ends north of Austin, the rugged limestone terrain continues to drop off to the blackland prairie to the east along the I-35 corridor through Waco and north to Dallas.

Because the best prospects for whitewater occur where streams cut through rock at a significant angle or gradient, the most likely places for Texas whitewater are at the edge of the Llano Estacado and along the Balcones Escarpment. Unfortunately, I can only point to some possible runs that come off the Llano Estacado because I know of no one from the Lubbock area who has capitalized on the rare occasions when streams there flood.

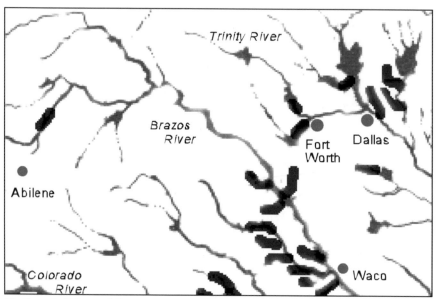

North-central Texas whitewater streams

For whitewater boaters in Texas, the Balcones Escarpment is the most significant geological feature in the state. Moisture from the Gulf of Mexico rising over the scarp often combines with colder air from the west and north to produce heavy thunderstorms. Rains that fall to the east of I-35 create few paddling opportunities. But when flooding occurs west of I-35 (north and west of Austin and San Antonio), whitewater conditions improve appreciably. The same is true for some of the streams around Dallas–Fort Worth and west of Waco.

Because most Texas whitewater paddlers live near Dallas–Fort Worth and Austin, most of the urban streams discussed in this book are located in those two metropolitan areas. No doubt, as San Antonio boaters begin to explore some of their local creeks, they will discover the same kinds of possibilities found on runs frequented by their northern neighbors. I have therefore included several creeks near San Antonio that promise to attract paddlers' attention in the future.

Winter and spring storms bring the rivers up. Occasional downpours and hurricanes during the summer and fall—and, every few years, El Niño—also help out. Dam-controlled rivers (e.g., the West and Clear Forks of the Trinity River, Denton Creek, the Brazos River, the North Fork of the San Gabriel River, the Colorado River, and the lower Guadalupe River) sometimes provide enough flow for playing. In addition, the spring-fed San Marcos River runs year-round for beginners and those who are desperate to be on moving water. The drainage areas of most free-flowing streams in Texas are too small and the rainfall too sporadic to provide a constant runnable level for whitewater.

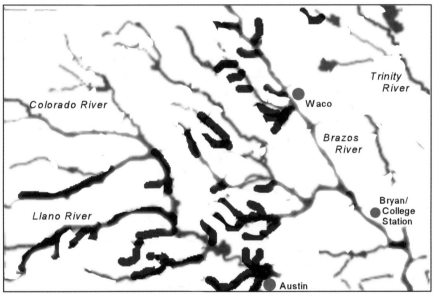

Central Texas whitewater streams

With a few exceptions, the gradient for the runs described in this book ranges from about 8 ft/mi to 30 ft/mi. Experienced whitewater boaters would consider gradients in this range exceedingly low, but an increase in water flow generally makes the runs worthwhile and provides an opportunity for playing. In most Texas limestone, sandstone, or composite river beds, water flow has not cut down through the rock as much as it has worn away the layers of stone to form ledges, pourovers, and occasionally channels and potholes. When higher water levels occur in those places (e.g., on the Llano, Pedernales, Blanco, and Brazos Rivers), interesting features can appear. When some impoundments overflow (e.g., the West Fork of the Trinity River at Lake Worth, the South Prong of Waxahachie Creek at Lake Waxahachie, and the Colorado River at Lake Buchanan), things get really interesting in their spillways.

In rare instances (e.g., Crabapple Creek), streams cut through granite instead of the limestone that typifies Hill Country river bottoms. When that happens, the gradient can be as high as 100 ft/mi. But such runs in Texas are as rare as hens' teeth, and only truly committed paddlers would run the gauntlet of hassles associated with getting on them.

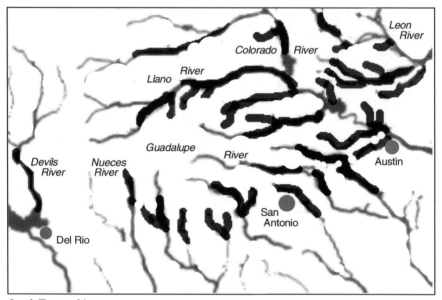

South Texas whitewater streams

The streams included in this book are arranged according to river drainages. Since the headwaters of different drainage areas are sometimes closer to one another than are stretches of the same river, I have provided maps to show nearby runs. Because much of the usefulness of a book like this depends on making decisions about where to go based on rainfall, I organized the book by region rather than alphabetically. This way of listing streams might also encourage boaters to paddle lesser-known creeks.

Undoubtedly, worthwhile streams are not on my list simply because I am unaware of them or because they have only isolated features that would be of interest to whitewater enthusiasts. Numerous spots exist throughout the state where ledges two or three feet high create small surfing holes at the right water level. Three of these appear on the Sabine River in East Texas: one below SH 42 west of Longview, another below US 79 near Carthage, and a third three miles downstream from the Toledo Bend Reservoir. Similar ledges can be found on the Neches River four miles east of US 69 near Woodville, and twice on the San Antonio River in the three miles upstream from Falls City.

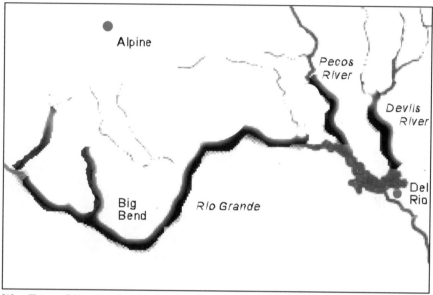

West Texas whitewater streams

Sometimes, as with Crystal Falls on the Clear Fork of the Brazos River north of Breckenridge, ledges can be up to five feet high and thus are true falls. But more often than not, they are the only thing of interest to whitewater paddlers for miles.

In the end, most of the information in this book is intended to help you not only enjoy the runs but also explore new ones. I hope you let me know about what you discover so that I can include it in future editions.

Explanation of the Format

The whitewater runs herein described range from multi-day stretches to play spots for surfing or practicing squirt moves or cartwheels on eddy lines. Each description begins with an overview of the location, gradient, drainage, and difficulty. Different water levels can transform some of these streams dramatically, making it almost impossible to provide detailed accounts of what to expect. Use the flow information to determine the possibility of whitewater on the run.

Of course, the amount of water needed to float down a river is much less than that needed to create interesting whitewater conditions; therefore, the minimum water levels or flow rates will appear high to leisure boaters. If you are interested in a float trip or are just beginning to develop whitewater skills, you will probably want to paddle at lower water levels than recommended or avoid the run entirely.

Carolyn Allbritton carves across a surfing wave on the Dry Frio River

Maps. New roads are constantly being built and old ones are sometimes renumbered. The information included in my maps provides a rough guide to help you get to streams. For more detail consult the most recent edition of *The Roads of Texas*, an atlas prepared by the Texas A&M University Cartographics Laboratory and based mostly on 1:100,000 maps (remote areas in West Texas are based on 1:250,000 maps). It tries to identify every dirt road, low-water bridge, rural cemetery, and road crossing cattle guard in the state. Unfortunately, it leaves out some roads that are included in the less detailed *Texas Atlas and Gazetteer* published by DeLorme (1995), which is based on 1:250,000 maps. The DeLorme atlas also includes 1:50,000 street maps of 100 cities in the state. With both atlases, you can find your way to anywhere in the state.

All of my maps are aligned north-south. Although most streams in Texas flow from west to east or north to south, there are exceptions; check the description. Potential put-in spots are marked with dark arrows pointing to the stream, and takeouts have dark arrows pointing away from the stream. Combination put-in/takeout spots are marked with double-pointing dark arrows. I occasionally use light arrows to point out certain river features or geographic locations. Standard road abbreviations include

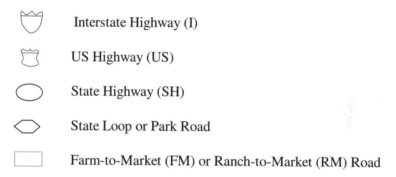

Interstate Highway (I)

US Highway (US)

State Highway (SH)

State Loop or Park Road

Farm-to-Market (FM) or Ranch-to-Market (RM) Road

Farm-to-market roads are generally located east of Interstate 35, and ranch-to-market roads, or simply ranch roads (RR), are usually found west of Interstate 35. However, the Texas Department of Transportation does not have a specific policy about how these roads are designated. I usually refer to all such roads as farm-to-market. In my maps, numbers with no letter designation refer to county roads.

River Gauges. In addition to facts about gradient, rapids, and access, most whitewater paddlers want to know how to determine whether a river is up. Information about water quality or scenery is fine but irrelevant if there is no water. Appendix A provides map data and lists Internet sites with information on stream conditions, including a table (arranged by county) of whitewater streams that should be checked after heavy rains. Appendix B lists the streamflow gauges on rivers and creeks and identifies Web sites where those gauge readings are found.

Finding New Whitewater Streams

Few boaters have been able to take advantage of the rare occasions when some of the whitewater creeks I list are runnable. As the numbers of skilled boaters in the state increase, more will have the chance to investigate hitherto unrun stretches.

Most of the so-called unrun streams I mention have been paddled by someone without whitewater experience or equipment. Locals often tell about growing up near a creek and paddling it, frequently losing a johnboat or canoe in the process. Their description of a run usually leaves something to be desired in terms of accurate information, but it hints at what to expect.

Common sense would indicate that if a river (e.g., the Llano) is running at several thousand cubic feet per second (cfs), then some of its feeder creeks and tributaries—which need only a few hundred cfs to be runnable—might be up as well. Knowing where to find the best options is important. That is why I have included maps of areas where streams of different drainages are close to one another.

Kayakers at play below Longhorn Dam on the Colorado River in Austin. © David Abel

Although I list only three spillway runs, I suspect that the next frontier for hair boaters will be those steep and turbulent diversions around dams. Because owner-operators of big dams and reservoirs often prohibit access to spillways, I anticipate that some of the best chances for interesting spillway runs will be found at the midsize lakes that pockmark the state's navigable streams. Since we are cursed with long periods of dry weather, and since such runs are based on extensive dry-bed scouting, checking out these runs give us something to do while we await the next El Niño.

My information is based on a number of sources, including hearsay and speculation. Sometimes boaters on a main stream will notice a creek coming in that seems to have enough water to paddle. But by the time they determine whether access and gradient issues would warrant their checking the creek out, it is usually too low.

To allow boaters to make informed decisions more quickly, I have included hard-to-find information that is usually buried in the Government Documents section of only a few libraries.

For example, to find out about the size of drainage areas for streams, I have reviewed a number of reports issued by the U.S. Geological Survey (USGS) in cooperation with the Texas Water Commission and its subsequent incarnations, the Texas Water Development Board and the Texas Department of Water Resources. These reports often provide information about feeder creeks in a river drainage. Without these reports we would not know which creeks drain areas large enough to justify scrutiny during periods of heavy rain.

I also studied topographic maps for runs that look promising because of their gradient. Unlike most boaters, who do not have the opportunity to use a complete collection of detailed topo maps, over the years I have been able to consult the holdings of the map room at the Sterling Evans Library at Texas A&M University.

By combining this data with drainage and access information, I have tried to identify streams that will be targets for the next generation of paddlers. I want this book to serve not only as a guide of known streams but as a resource for future exploration.

River Ratings and Classifications

The issue of rating rivers and rapids has a wonderful history and has occasioned marvelous displays of rationalization, bravado, and genuine concern for those less familiar with the nuances of the system. With improvements in paddling techniques, equipment, and experience, the limit of what is navigable has expanded and has influenced how rivers and rapids are rated. In addition, the exploding interest in creek boating has forced many whitewater paddlers to reconsider the standard characteristics for rating the difficulty of rapids.

According to the 1998 American Whitewater scale of river difficulty

- Class I (easy) refers to fast-moving water with riffles or small waves and few if any obstructions.

- Class II (novice) covers small rapids with waves of up to two feet, few large rocks, and wide, clear channels.

- Class III (intermediate) includes rapids with three-foot irregular waves, small hydraulics, strong eddies, and narrow passages requiring complex maneuvering.

- Class IV (advanced) rapids have constricted passages that require precise moves in very turbulent water, four- to six-foot waves, boiling eddies, dangerous hydraulics and undercut rocks; scouting is necessary and rescue is often difficult. A strong Eskimo roll is highly recommended.

- Class V (expert) includes long, difficult, violent rapids with highly congested routes, six- to eight-foot waves, strong currents, and deep hydraulics that are life-threatening in the event of a mishap. Class V is an open-ended, multiple level scale designated 5.0, 5.1, 5.2, etc., with each level being an order of magnitude more difficult than the last.

- Class VI rapids have almost never been attempted and are extremely difficult, unpredictable, and dangerous. Consequences of error are very severe and rescue may be impossible. For teams of experts only at favorable water levels taking all precautions.

Whitewater paddlers often describe river difficulty less in terms of some imagined objective standard than in terms of comparisons with other well-known runs. Instead of speaking of class I to class VI as if such a scale has been developed apart from real rivers, most boaters today discuss the skills needed for certain runs by relating them to the skills needed to paddle other known benchmark streams competently. That is the policy adopted in the 1998 American Whitewater safety code, and I have followed it here.

For example, most whitewater paddlers agree that the Nantahala River in North Carolina is class II (with one class III rapid): occasional swift current with few obstacles, but nothing that requires any real paddling competence, as evidenced by the numerous canoeing tourists and inner-tubers. However, it would be odd to find inner-tubers on class III+ runs such as Tennessee's Ocoee River (1,200–1,600 cfs) or Colorado's Brown's Canyon of the Arkansas River (2,500 cfs). Where proper equipment and skill are necessary to avoid mishap, we begin to see class III.

First drop of Pedernales Falls

Using current criteria, it would be difficult to classify most Texas whitewater as anything more than class II. Even when streams are up, their lack of gradient is reason enough for not inflating their difficulty level. Of course, ledges and low-head dams make certain runs more hazardous for tubers and beginners, and a rain-swollen river can be dangerous for anyone without the necessary skills to paddle it. But it would be misleading to rate a river where drunken tubers bounce gleefully down rapids (as on the lower Guadalupe) as anything more than a class II when compared with rivers in other states.

Assuredly, some Texans may feel slighted by my low ratings or think that I am using criteria endorsed only by expert decked boaters. I can only reply that river rating is subjective and that I have relied on benchmarks identified by members of American Whitewater. I try to give an up-to-date rating assessment by placing my remarks in contexts similar to those described in recent works such as *Colorado Rivers and Creeks* (1995) by Gordon Banks and Dave Eckardt and *Southeastern Whitewater* (1995) by Monte Smith. Anyone who wonders why I am stingy in handing out class IV ratings for Texas streams should try to find anything in Texas like section IV of the Chattooga River (South Carolina) or the Numbers on the Arkansas River (Colorado).

Twelve-year-old Jared Leon punches a frothy hole on the Lampasas River. Photo by Paulo Pinto, courtesy Bill Leon

My classification of each stream refers to the run in general. Because changes in water level can affect classification, I sometimes indicate a range (e.g., II–III). A plus (+) or minus (–) indicates how the run or rapid compares with others. If there is a particular rapid or drop that is more difficult than the run in general, I make note of it in parentheses.

Safety

As exhilarating as whitewater paddling can be, it is also an inherently risky and even dangerous activity. It should be pursued only by those with the equipment and expertise necessary to handle the difficulties that inevitably arise in a wild and changing environment. As even well-seasoned paddlers discover, a class II river can present more than they can handle if they are not vigilant.

- Always wear a helmet and life vest and have flotation in your boat.

- In cold weather or cold water conditions, anticipate getting wet and wear appropriate gear to keep out water and maintain warmth.

- Have throw ropes, spare paddles, and other rescue items. Sooner or later the hassle of their weight will be offset by an emergency.

- Keep an eye on those with whom you boat; they might need your help or you might need theirs. Don't paddle alone.

- Familiarize yourself well with the river before putting on. Once on the river, don't hesitate to get out of your boat to scout obstacles (especially low-head dams), and don't hesitate to portage if things just don't feel right.

- Watch out for barbed-wire fences, and never cut or destroy such barriers (even if they are illegally stretched across a stream). Because most barbed-wire fences (especially those separated by sticks) are not anchored in the river bed, you usually can float up to them and simply lift them to pass under. Embedded metal-post fences are more dangerous. Go over or around them if possible.

- Avoid confrontations with landowners.

Note: the author and the publisher assume no responsibility for users of this book. Neither the author nor the publisher can be held responsible for accidents incurred on any stream or in getting to and from any river or creek. This book does not advocate paddling any of these runs. It identifies the opportunities available to paddlers in the state and assumes that boaters are familiar with the risks and are liable for their own actions.

Texas Law

If you paddle whitewater in Texas, you'd better know something about the law, politics, and landowners. Even if the law is on your side, that is probably not enough because law enforcement officers, county prosecutors, and government officials often mistakenly think that the right to own private property overrides all other claims of use.

Indeed, for some landowners, any encroachment on private property is grounds for taking the law into their own hands. Harassment, arrest, and threats of force against river runners are not uncommon—even when local sheriffs or deputies have been informed by the Office of the Attorney General (AG) of the public's right to paddle stretches of river or of the illegality of fencing off rivers or access points.

Bruce Tate on Bull Creek in Austin

Since the AG's opinion does not have the force of a judicial judgment, many landowners would rather risk a loss in court than acknowledge a right of passage. Governmental representatives (e.g., sheriffs and county attorneys) would rather risk reversal of a county court judgment by a higher court than alienate the people who elected them by not charging a boater with trespass. They know that just the threat of litigation is enough to dissuade most whitewater paddlers from putting on a river.

Because so many conflicting constituencies are at work, no one in any official administrative capacity wants to get into hot water for saying anything that could be taken as clear or definitive. Official publications (such as the 1974 *Analysis of Texas Waterways*) are filled with comments such as "The Texas Parks and Wildlife Department accepts no responsibility, either expressed or implied, for any legal ramifications occurring from the use of this publication by any person other than waterway analysis purposes."

Despite such reluctance, the Texas Parks and Wildlife Department (TPWD) has published guidelines ("for general information only") in *Floating Texas Waterways* (1990) regarding public access and legal rights. These guidelines serve as a starting point.

The guidelines, augmented with information that relates to issues of access and use, include the following:

- Boaters should respect private property adjacent to public waterways. Private landowners must respect the public's right to travel, float, fish, or recreate on state-owned (navigable) streams.

- A stream is navigable by law if it averages thirty feet in width between the riverbanks from its mouth up to the stretch in question. With a few rare exceptions, the beds of navigable streams are publicly owned, and the public has a right to use these streambeds, including sandbars or islands. Private landowners may not erect fences or other structures that prevent unimpeded travel on public streams. Even in those instances where the bed of a navigable stream is privately owned, the public has a right to float the stream because the water is in the public domain.

- The public has no legal right to use non-navigable streams. Although the water of even non-navigable streams is public property, the beds may be privately owned, and property owners can prevent public use of such streams. A person commits trespass if he or she enters or remains on private property without effective consent or is notified (e.g., by fences or posted signs) that entry is forbidden; or receives notice to depart but fails to do so. (As you might suspect, the question of the navigability of a stream sometimes requires judicial resolution.)

- The public does not have the right to trespass on private land to reach a navigable (public) waterway. Access to public waterways may be gained from publicly owned areas like highway rights-of-way (which vary from ten feet to more than thirty feet) or public parks. One way to tell the width of the right-of-way is to note where landowners put their fences (though that is not always a surefire indication of where the property line is, since some landowners encroach on public property).

Rick Beale side-surfs on the Pedernales River at 20,000 cfs. © David Abel

- Parking regulations are subject to change. Where local authorities have posted No Parking signs (even with no justification other than that the landowner wants to discourage paddlers from accessing a navigable stream), obey the signs. No Trespassing or Posted signs do not have the same legitimacy, nor do barbed-wire or other fences necessarily mean that access to the stream is legally prohibited.

- Although the public has the right to travel on the state's public waterways, most of the shorelines of these streams are privately owned. The dividing line between public and private ownership of the land bordering a navigable waterway is the "gradient boundary." That is the point midway between the lowest and highest levels of the "cut bank"—namely, the point midway between where the streambed meets the bank and where the stream would overflow the banks in flood. Above that dividing line is private property.

As is indicated in painstaking detail in Joe Riddell's "Overview of Laws Regarding the Navigation of Texas Streams" (appendix C), the nuances in meaning about access and navigability have kept the courts and state agencies humming for decades. Throughout the state, landowners have built fences across navigable rivers, put up No Trespassing signs at legal access points, run barbed-wire fences across public rights-of-way to bridge abutments, and persuaded local authorities to discourage legitimate recreational use of streams (especially when flows are high enough for whitewater).

Admittedly, the typical reasons given to justify such practices—to contain livestock, to prevent littering and destruction of private property, to avoid confrontations between the public and landowners about disputes on how to apply the law, to protect people from being injured in flooding conditions—are beside the point as far as most whitewater boaters are concerned. Fences, dams, and low-water crossings are often not unlike natural obstacles such as downed trees, ledges, and pourovers: they are part of paddling. If someone needs to portage around a danger, the law recognizes such passage as a legitimate defense against a charge of trespass. But the law is one thing and locally elected officials or gun-toting landowners are another. Know your rights, but be prepared to deal with much more than terminal hydraulics when paddling in Texas.

David Abel lines up his raft in Upper Madison Rapid in the Lower Canyons of the Rio Grande. Photo by Joe Riddell. © David Abel

One final note: The fact that a river or creek is listed in this book is not a guarantee that everyone acknowledges the right of boaters to paddle on it. Users should consider the legal ambiguities regarding river access issues and, as in the case of safety, recognize that they alone are legally liable for their actions.

PART TWO

~

Trinity River Drainage

Seventeen-foot waterfall on the spillway of the South Prong of Waxahachie Creek. Courtesy Bryan Craven

Trinity River Drainage

FOR MOST OF ITS 550-MILE JOURNEY through East Texas, the Trinity River has no whitewater. But on its forks and feeder creeks around Fort Worth and Dallas, there are short stretches and play spots that attract paddlers after heavy rains or during dam releases.

The West Fork and the Clear Fork come into the Dallas–Fort Worth metroplex from the west, and the Elm Fork and East Fork have their headwaters north of Dallas. All join in Dallas to form the Trinity. In contrast to the West Fork and Clear Fork, the Elm Fork and East Fork generally do not have the creekbeds or gradient to make them appealing to whitewater boaters. But some of the creeks that feed into them have characteristics that make fun runs.

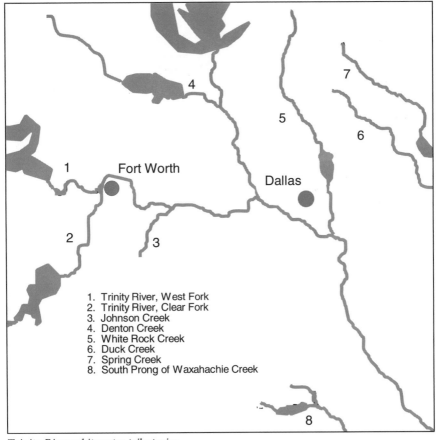

1. Trinity River, West Fork
2. Trinity River, Clear Fork
3. Johnson Creek
4. Denton Creek
5. White Rock Creek
6. Duck Creek
7. Spring Creek
8. South Prong of Waxahachie Creek

Trinity River whitewater tributaries

Above the impoundments created by the dams are places yet to be paddled that probably contain an undiscovered gem. If their creekbeds and whitewater features are anything like what one finds below the dams, they promise to provide boaters with a new set of interesting runs.

Entrance to the falls on the South Prong of Waxahachie Creek. Courtesy Bryan Craven

West Fork of the Trinity River

Run: Lake Worth Spillway to River Oaks Blvd. (Old US 183)		
Location: Fort Worth	*County*: Tarrant	*Drainage*: 2,064 mi² *Length*: 2½ miles
Gradient: 10 ft/mi *Class*: II+ (V)	*Gauge*: West Fork of the Trinity at Fort Worth, 700 cfs (1.6') minimum	

The West Fork of the Trinity begins 145 miles to the west of Fort Worth in Archer County. It is dammed three times along its course (Lake Bridgeport, Eagle Mountain Lake, and Lake Worth). As in most areas where dams are built, the highest gradient and best chance for play spots are just below each dam.

When Lake Worth is between six inches and one foot over its normal 594-foot conservation-pool elevation, the spillway itself becomes a hair run, dropping forty-five feet in less than one-quarter mile (or 225 ft/mi). At more than a foot over, the spillway run turns nasty due to the hydraulic at the six-foot drop at the bottom. When the lake is 2½ to 3 feet over the spillway level, there are fantastic surfing waves, holes, a vertical ledge where the river drops up to six feet—and some deadly hydraulics—between the spillway and River Oaks Boulevard. At 2½ feet over, there is a sweet surfing spot just above River Oaks Boulevard. At three feet over, a great surfing wave and ender spot upstream of Meandering Road are easily accessible from Meandering Road on the south side of the river.

For the lake level, call the Corps of Engineers at (817) 978-2214 or check their Web site (http://swf66.swf-wc.usace.army.mil).

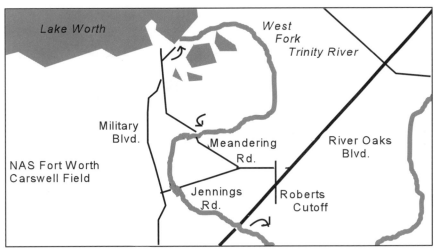

West Fork of the Trinity River

Clear Fork of the Trinity River

Run: Bryant Irvin Road to University Drive		
Location: Fort Worth	*County*: Tarrant	*Drainage*: 431 mi² *Length*: 3½ miles
Gradient: 7 ft/mi *Class*: II+	*Gauge*: Clear Fork of the Trinity at Fort Worth, 700–3,000 cfs (9.7–11')	

Not far south of the West Fork is the Clear Fork, a shorter and smaller branch of the Trinity. Its upper stretches have gravel bottoms that are promising at high water, but most of its drop in gradient is negated by dams that create Lake Weatherford and Benbrook Lake. Below Benbrook the Clear Fork joins the West Fork in Fort Worth.

Before the Clear Fork meets the West Fork, it crashes its way out of Benbrook Lake down to some of the best play spots in the Trinity drainage. From Bryant Irvin Road (River Park) to South University Drive near the Fort Worth Zoo (Forest Park), the river provides numerous opportunities to polish your surfing skills. In the first mile of this 3½-mile run, play spots abound at 700–800 cfs. Above 1,500 cfs those spots turn into big waves. However, four dams—some up to eight feet high—can create scary hydraulics at high water. Be especially careful of the dam at Hulen Street, midway in the run.

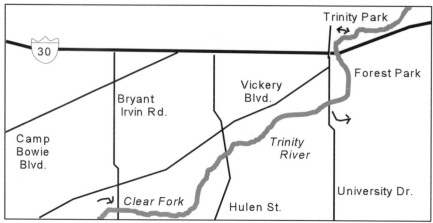

Clear Fork of the Trinity River

When the flow rate is 3,000 cfs, take out at University and head north to Trinity Park just a mile downstream to avoid a bad twenty-foot dam one-half mile past University. In the park near the site of the annual Mayfest celebration (just north of I-30) are two good surfing holes created by low-water rock crossings separated by a few hundred yards.

To find out about releases from the dam, consult the Corps of Engineers Web site (http://swf66.swf-wc.usace.army.mil). Otherwise refer to the USGS stream-flow page.

Johnson Creek

Run: Meadowbrook Park to Great Southwest Parkway		
Location: Arlington	*County*: Tarrant	*Drainage*: 25 mi² *Length*: 3½ miles
Gradient: 20 ft/mi *Class*: II (III)	*Gauge*: None; look for heavy rain at the Lake Arlington gauge	

For anyone who has ever wondered what else is on Johnson Creek besides the ten-foot falls beneath the Shock Wave roller coaster at Six Flags over Texas, the answer is this: perhaps not enough for the hassles you face. The falls have been run at optimal levels, but you will probably incur the wrath of the Six Flags security personnel when you stop to scout the falls.

Bryan Craven, Wade Locker, and Bill Anton on Johnson Creek downstream from falls. Photo by Darrell Byers, courtesy Bryan Craven

The run between Meadowbrook Park and Richard Green Park (formerly Punch Wright Park) includes several pipelines that cross the creek and have to be portaged. A nasty dam near the Ballpark in Arlington has created a large lake, and two other dams occur at the Great Southwest Golf Course. Near the golf course there are some small drops. The best one is a quarter-mile past the

golf course, where a fast little rapid provides some compensation for everything you have to endure to reach it.

Although there is no gauge for the creek, you can check local rainfall on the gauge at Lake Arlington Dam three miles west of the creek headwaters.

Bryan Craven at Johnson Creek Falls, Six Flags.
Photo by Darrell Byers, courtesy Bryan Craven

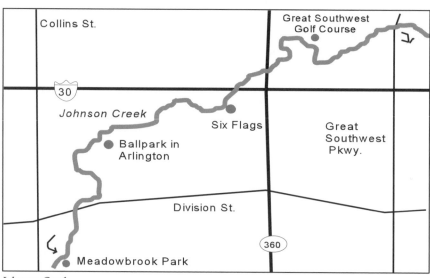

Johnson Creek

Denton Creek

Run: Play spot below Grapevine Dam		
Location: Northeast of Fort Worth	County: Tarrant	Drainage: 705 mi² Length: 50 yards
Gradient: Drops five feet Class: II+		Gauge: Grapevine Dam release, 650–2,000 cfs

The surfing hole/wave below Grapevine Dam is the play spot of choice in the area. Between 650–800 cfs, a wonderful thirty-foot-wide forgiving horseshoe wave forms; 700 cfs is optimal. Above 800 cfs, things start to get pushy and the hole is challenging. New waves start appearing above 1,500 cfs; and above 2,000 cfs the play spots are only for the big dogs.

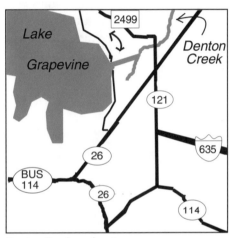

Denton Creek surf spot

Access to the creek below the dam is down an inclined quarter-mile road at the Grapevine Golf Course on the north side of the creek. A gate at the head of the road is usually locked after 11 A.M. If you get there earlier, you will often find it open; you can drive down to the creek to drop off your boat. Always return your vehicle to outside the gate to avoid being locked in. After playing, you face a trek back uphill. Inventive paddlers have been seen hauling their boats on all kinds of contraptions, including an airport baggage cart.

Information about dam releases can be found at the Corps of Engineers Web site (http://swf66.swf-wc.usace.army.mil) or on their recording: phone (817) 481-3576, then press 1.

During periods of heavy rain when things change hourly, consult the USGS Web site (which is updated every few hours). Although the USGS site does not have a gauge for below the dam, you can estimate the flow by subtracting the Lewisville reading of the Elm Fork from the reading for Denton Creek at Carrollton and then adding the flow of Denton Creek at Justin.

Late every morning the dam's release is also posted at gopher://twister. sbs.ohio-state.edu:70/0/wxascii/rivercond/riverUS11.KFTW. For weekend releases, check the same Web address but change US11 to US22. Because weekend projections are based on data compiled on Wednesday morning, things can change quickly if it rains heavily between Wednesday and Saturday.

White Rock Creek

Run: Belt Line Road to Forest Lane		
Location: North Dallas	*County*: Dallas	*Drainage*: 41 mi² *Length*: 3½ miles
Gradient: 10 ft/mi *Class*: II–III	*Gauge*: White Rock Creek at Greenville Avenue, at least 700 cfs (74.6')	

A perennial favorite of Dallas area paddlers, White Rock Creek draws hordes of boaters every time north Dallas gets a gully washer. Waves and holes (with names like the Dragon's Lair and Big Rock) can sometimes get very big, so the creek's reputation for munching novices and intermediates is well deserved. Experienced paddlers in the area, though, think of the creek as a godsend.

Tim Doogs surfs a big wave on White Rock Creek. Courtesy Bryan Craven

North of Belt Line Road is one of the creek's first noteworthy features, a marginally runnable eight-foot dam at Prestonwood Country Club. Several fun rapids take shape from there down past Fields Park and Valley View Park to I-635 (LBJ Parkway). The dams along the creek are runnable at certain water levels. Check their status from the bike path that parallels almost the entire length of the run. One of the best rapids can be seen just upstream of I-635.

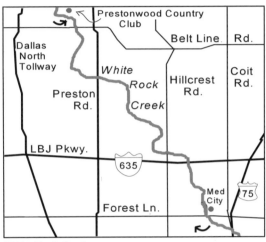

White Rock Creek

The White Rock trailhead off Hillcrest Road (just north of LBJ Parkway) is the put-in for the most commonly paddled portion of the creek. This 1½-mile stretch contains the best rapids and cuts through Anderson-Bonner Park leading to the Midway, the best part of the creek. There, a fun play hole is followed by nice surfing waves north of Forest Lane (at the Humana Hospital Medical City). Below that, a huge diagonal forms as the creek goes into a concrete-lined channel that speeds the water up and sends you merrily on to the takeout.

Duck Creek

Run: North Shiloh Road to South Garland Avenue		
Location: Garland	County: Dallas	Drainage: 32 mi² Length: 2 miles
Gradient: 11 ft/mi Class: II–III	Gauge: None; use Rowlett Creek near Sachse, 1,000 cfs (9.9') minimum	

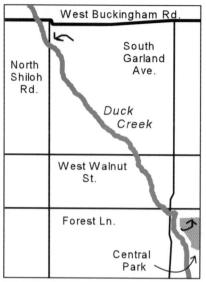

Duck Creek

Before Duck Creek passes through Garland's Central Park and is transformed into an irregularly paved ditch, it cuts through remote packed clay deposits to form waves, holes, and play spots galore. So few people have paddled the Duck after heavy rains that it is difficult to get a sense of all that it promises. The stretch described here is the only part of the creek that has been run so far. It is possible that the rechanneling in the mile downstream from Central Park to Oden Park might create some extra play spots. As more folks learn of the upper two miles, the Duck will likely become a popular destination for north Dallas paddlers.

Spring Creek

Run: Renner Road to Jupiter Road		
Location: Richardson, north of Dallas	Counties: Collin, Dallas	Drainage: 45 mi² Length: 3 miles
Gradient: 11 ft/mi Class: II	Gauge: None; use Rowlett Creek near Sachse, 1,000 cfs (9.9') minimum	

Just south of the intersection of US 75 and SH 190 (George Bush Parkway) is a greenbelt along Spring Creek, a gravel- and rock-bottomed stream that only recently has attracted boaters. Its drainage area is small, so it rises and falls quickly. State highway maps mistake it for Pittman Creek, one of its tributaries.

Beneath the Renner Road bridge put-in is a great surfing wave after heavy rains. It also has good play spots in the 1½ miles from there to Foxboro

Spring Creek

Park, east of North Plano Road. A paved hiking trail parallels the creek from Renner to Overlook Park one-half mile downstream (east) of Foxboro Park. To add another mile, take out at Jupiter Road.

Lagniappe: Across the creek from Foxboro Park, at the turn for Overlook Park, is Spring Creek Farm. There you can go on tours to see how Owens Country Sausage is made.

South Prong of Waxahachie Creek

Run: Lake Waxahachie spillway to Reagor Springs		
Location: South of Waxahachie	*County*: Ellis	*Drainage*: 31 mi² *Length*: 2½ miles
Gradient: ⅓ mile at 150 ft/mi; 2 miles at 10 ft/mi *Class*: III (IV–VI)	*Gauge*: None; use Mountain Creek at Venus, 200 cfs (6') minimum	

This hair run begins with 100 yards of screaming turbulence followed by two miles of cool-down. It is also another one of those runs that can appear and disappear in a few hours. Within a few minutes it can change from a low-water bounce (class III) over ledges to a class VI experience in terror.

Most of the time the spillway is bone dry, but after heavy rains water pours over the spillway at Lake Waxahachie, an impoundment on the South Prong of Waxahachie Creek. Where FM 877 crosses the dam, the spillway channel is 100 feet wide. From there the water rushes downstream around a bend and narrows to fifteen yards. Out of sight from the bridge, the creek crashes down a twelve-foot slope over two six-foot ledges and a seventeen-

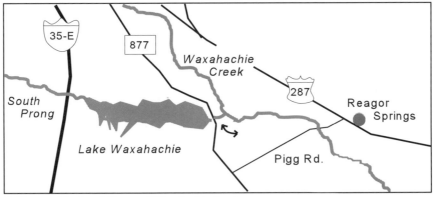

Spillway of the South Prong of Waxahachie Creek

Wade Locker runs the first big drop of Waxahachie Creek's South Prong spillway. Courtesy Bryan Craven

foot waterfall into a pool—all in a total of fifty yards. One boater who has run it at a moderate (class IV–V) level calls it "awesome."

Below the second big drop, the South Prong continues for one-half mile before meeting Waxahachie Creek, a narrow stream that drops 10 ft/mi for two miles down to Pigg Road (a.k.a. Old Reagor Springs Road). Rather than worrying about whether Waxahachie Creek is legally navigable, you should instead get permission from the landowner to take out on the South Prong below the last drop of the spillway.

PART THREE

~

Brazos River Drainage

Going for a screw-up at Hidalgo Falls on the Brazos River. © *David Abel*

Brazos River Drainage

THE BRAZOS RIVER DRAINS MORE than 42,000 square miles and runs 923 miles from the confluence of the Double Mountain Fork and Salt Fork north of Abilene to where it empties into the Gulf of Mexico south of Galveston. It meanders and takes on whitewater features only where the riverbed goes over rare, small rocky drops. Three major impoundments (Possum Kingdom, Granbury, and Whitney) control flows above Waco and often determine whether there is enough water for play spots downriver, such as Hidalgo Falls.

Most whitewater opportunities in the Brazos drainage fall into three categories:

- tributaries northwest of Waco (e.g., the Paluxy, the North Bosque)
- feeder streams of the Little River (a Brazos tributary) south and west of Temple (e.g., the Lampasas, the San Gabriel)
- play spots on the Brazos itself, where it crosses rock outcrops (e.g., Port Sullivan, Hidalgo Falls).

All have the limestone or bedrock bottoms and gradient that create whitewater conditions when heavy rains occur.

The exceptions to this general characterization occur where the upper forks of the Brazos slice through the Caprock or High Plains (Llano Estacado) Escarpment between Lubbock and Abilene. To my knowledge, none of these streams has been explored at runnable levels. Even when potential put-ins have sufficient water, much of the flow might seep underground before it reaches the next access point.

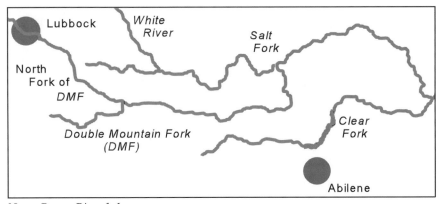

Upper Brazos River forks

For example, the North Fork of the Double Mountain Fork of the Brazos River, just east of Lubbock, cuts down through the Caprock Escarpment of the Llano Estacado in Yellow House Canyon. Although it generally has some flow at a potential put-in north of Slaton, topo maps indicate that the riverbed is replaced by sandy washes between that point and the next road crossing twenty-four miles downstream.

At high water the North Fork and the Salt Fork might have some interesting features, such as Silver Falls, a ten-foot drop on the White River east of Crosbyton. But until some local paddler investigates them, we can only imagine what they offer.

Clear Fork of the Brazos River

Run: US 180 to SH 6 (Lueders)		
Location: North of Abilene	*Counties*: Throckmorton, Shackelford	*Drainage*: 2,250 mi² *Length*: 5 miles
Gradient: 6 ft/mi *Class*: I (perhaps one IV)	*Gauge*: Clear Fork of Brazos at Nugent, 400 cfs (4.1') minimum	

Although the Clear Fork of the Brazos does not cut through the Llano Estacado Escarpment, it does have a drop that shows that even the area around Abilene warrants further exploration. I include it less as a whitewater run than a place that hints at the prospects of the region.

Getting there requires paddling across four miles of Lake Shackelford

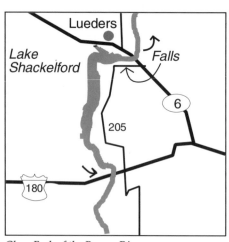

Clear Fork of the Brazos River

after putting in at US 180 south of Lueders. Immediately past a small dam downstream are two stair-step falls that together drop twenty feet.

Although I have not paddled this stretch or talked to anyone who has, I suspect that these ledges are intimidating at high water. Because the ledges are less than a mile from the takeout, it might be easier to paddle up to them along the banks if the water is not too high. The flat-water paddle across the lake may not be as tiresome at high water, and the drop itself could be interesting. Putting in at Cottonwood Creek in Lueders saves you the hassle of lake paddling and is only three-quarters of a mile upstream from the ledges.

For those interested in a remote, scenic multi-day trip, the eighty miles downstream from Lueders looks tailor-made. The river cuts through the remote terrain of small canyons and high bluffs at a leisurely gradient of 4 ft/mi. The only public access is just upstream from Fort Griffin State Park.

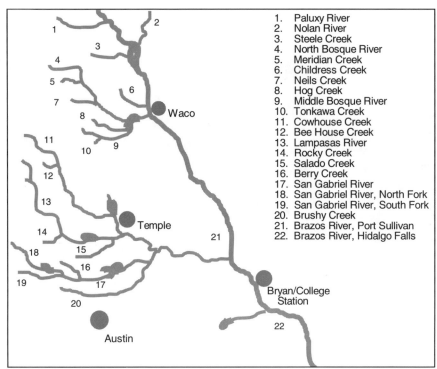

1. Paluxy River
2. Nolan River
3. Steele Creek
4. North Bosque River
5. Meridian Creek
6. Childress Creek
7. Neils Creek
8. Hog Creek
9. Middle Bosque River
10. Tonkawa Creek
11. Cowhouse Creek
12. Bee House Creek
13. Lampasas River
14. Rocky Creek
15. Salado Creek
16. Berry Creek
17. San Gabriel River
18. San Gabriel River, North Fork
19. San Gabriel River, South Fork
20. Brushy Creek
21. Brazos River, Port Sullivan
22. Brazos River, Hidalgo Falls

Lower Brazos River whitewater tributaries

Paluxy River

Run: Somervell CR 1008 to Glen Rose City Park		
Location: Southwest of Fort Worth	*County*: Somervell	*Drainage*: 410 mi² *Length*: 10 miles
Gradient: 11 ft/mi *Class*: II–III	*Gauge*: Paluxy at Glen Rose, 400 cfs (3.3') minimum	

The Paluxy River is formed by the confluence of its North and South Forks in Bluff Dale and flows only thirty-five miles before meeting the Brazos two miles past Glen Rose. At places it is 150 feet wide, but it often narrows to form excellent surfing waves (some up to four feet high). Immediately after heavy rains the water is murky; as the river level drops, the clear water reveals a limestone creekbed. Dinosaur tracks are visible near the banks of the river as it passes through Dinosaur Valley State Park (except at high water).

Roger Smith on the Paluxy River at 400 cfs

The most popular whitewater run includes many surfing waves, beginning with one on the river left side of the island at the put-in. Beginner surfers will find a good wave where the river makes a right turn at one of the park observation decks. Just downstream on river left is an ender wave near some dinosaur tracks. At moderate to high water flows, a river-wide hydraulic forms at the low-water crossing below the FM 205 bridge. Run it in the middle only if it has a pronounced tongue; otherwise, portage.

The best surfing waves and holes are between FM 205 and the takeout, especially one-quarter mile upstream from the SH 144 bridge. A low-head dam just upstream of the bridge can be grabby at times. To avoid it, run far left. Below the bridge are more surfing waves and holes. Those who want just one more wave to play on can find it at the takeout at Big Rock Park.

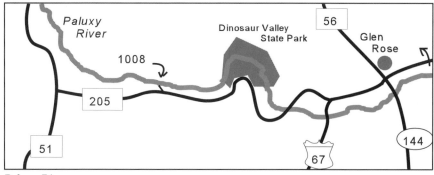

Paluxy River

Although the optimal level for playing is around 2,500 cfs, the Paluxy is a great place for fast surfing, 360s, and rodeo moves even at low flow levels. At 6,000 cfs most of the good spots are washed out, but a few big waves create opportunities for impressive enders.

Lagniappe: Shuttle bunnies (and boaters as well) who want to see the dinosaur tracks should go to the state park when the river is not high enough to run. Replicas of the tracks in the small park museum and the small shops in Glen Rose offer off-river diversions. Serious shoppers and antique enthusiasts prefer to spend the day in Granbury (seventeen miles north of Glen Rose).

Glen Rose native Clint Staples plays on the Paluxy River at 2,500 cfs

Nolan River

Run: SH 174 to Adair Spring Park		
Location: South of Cleburne	County: Hill	Drainage: 256 mi² Length: 6 miles
Gradient: 10 ft/mi Class: II	Gauge: Nolan River at Blum, 250 cfs (3.1') minimum; 1,000 cfs (4.5') maximum	

Most of the whitewater streams that feed the Brazos River flow in from the west. The Nolan River is an exception.

When the area east of the Paluxy (between Fort Worth and Waco) gets rain, the Nolan's hard-packed clay streambed sports several surfing spots and small ledges. South of Cleburne, down past Rio Vista, the river flows clear over gravel and broken clay. Three miles north of Blum the clay and gravel composites form more distinct features and create small rapids. A four-foot-high waterfall north of the heart of Blum is just downstream from Hill CR 1127. The streambed from Blum to the takeout on Rock Creek is solid and makes nice surfing waves when the river is up.

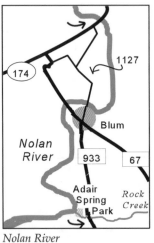

Nolan River

Take out at the FM 933 bridge over Rock Creek, a tributary of the Nolan. To reach the bridge, walk or paddle up the creek at Adair Spring Park. In the spring, locals park at the bridge and use the creek to access the river to catch sand bass making their way up from Lake Whitney to spawn.

Steele Creek

Run: Morgan to FM 56 (Lakeside Village)		
Location: South of Fort Worth	County: Bosque	Drainage: 60 mi² Length: 10 miles
Gradient: 17 ft/mi Class: Probably II+	Gauge: Paluxy River at Glen Rose, 3,000 cfs (6.8') minimum	

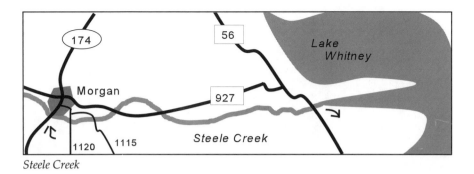

Steele Creek

Recently paddlers have started wondering what the Paluxy's smaller neighbor to the south, Steele Creek, might be like when heavy rains make the Paluxy a flushing torrent. Steele runs alongside a scenic ridge, and this suggests that there might be some interesting rock features that could translate into rapids when the creek is flowing. Springs in the area provide a small flow even during dry periods. One day when the Paluxy is almost washed out, some lucky boater will discover just what Steele has been doing upstream to create its rocky creekbed between Morgan and Lake Whitney.

The stream at the SH 174 put-in, like at the other road crossings, has the kind of bottom that generally guarantees surfing waves at high water. The bridge crossings at Bosque CR 1120 and CR 1115 are just low enough to present problems when you pass under them at high water. There is also a dam at the Steele Creek Ranch about halfway through the run.

To get to the bridges at CR 1120 and CR 1115, go east on Mary Street in Morgan and turn south on Shepherd Street (which becomes CR 1120).

North Bosque River

Run: Hico to Iredell		
Location: Hico, Iredell	*Counties*: Hamilton, Bosque	*Drainage*: 359 mi² *Length*: 14 miles
Gradient: 9 ft/mi *Class*: I–II	*Gauge*: North Bosque at Hico, 500 cfs (3') minimum	

The Bosque River is formed by the confluence of the North, Middle, and South Forks at Lake Waco. Neither the South Fork nor the stretch from Lake Waco Dam to the river's confluence with the Brazos is of real consequence. In contrast, the North Bosque and Middle Bosque and their tributaries have several whitewater runs.

North Bosque ledge upstream from the Iredell bridge at 15 cfs

With headwaters in north Erath County, the North Bosque is the longest (115 miles) of the forks of the Bosque. Like the Paluxy, the North Bosque is a play river only after heavy rains. Its small surfing spots provide a chance for beginners to practice whitewater basics. When the river floods and the rapids wash out, the tributaries offer more advanced paddlers some diversion.

Upstream from Hico and downstream from Iredell, the North Bosque has long stretches of flat water interrupted occasionally by ripples. Between Hico (City Park on Elm Street) and Iredell (FM 216) is the whitewater run, with the best play spots in the last six miles above Iredell (where the gradient increases to 11 ft/mi). Access this lower stretch from CR 110 south of CR 100B.

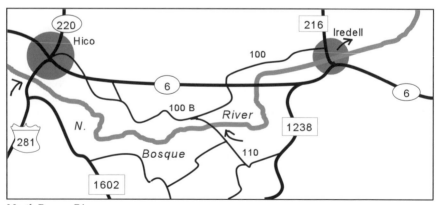

North Bosque River

If the water is high enough, there is an interesting zig-zag rapid two miles downstream from the lower put-in. A nice surfing wave can be found 200 yards upstream from the SH 6 crossing, and at low water there is a small but fun surfing hole below the SH 6 bridge. The most notable play feature on the run is a three-foot ledge that extends diagonally across the river one-quarter miles upstream from the Iredell takeout.

Lagniappe: Because of its antiques and crafts shops and live street music on Saturday nights, Hico is becoming a popular destination for weekenders from Dallas and Fort Worth. But don't go there expecting Pigeon Forge or Durango.

Meridian Creek

Run: Bosque CR 347 to SH 6		
Location: Northwest of Waco	*County*: Bosque	*Drainage*: 185 mi² *Length*: 8 miles
Gradient: 18 ft/mi *Class*: II	*Gauge*: North Bosque at Clifton, 2,000 cfs (5.6') minimum	

Meridian Creek is a tributary of the North Bosque. It has a few small ledges and some tight turns through boulders and trees, but it does not have much whitewater. Its gradient is spread out among jumbles of small rocks, and play spots are few and far between. Below the low-water crossing east of where Meridian and Spring Creeks come together (CR 347), there are two other crossings (CR 331 and CR 334) that divide the run into three parts. The middle part is the most scenic as it passes high bluffs west of Clifton.

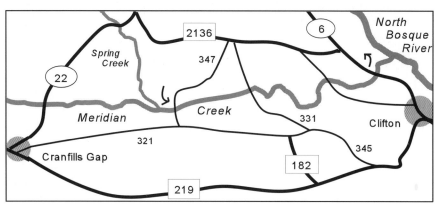

Meridian Creek

Childress Creek

Run: Cayote (FM 56) to FM 2490		
Location: Northwest of Waco	Counties: Bosque, McLennan	Drainage: 88 mi² Length: 17 miles
Gradient: 18 ft/mi Class: II–III		Gauge: Hog Creek near Crawford, 4.5' minimum

A small version of the Middle Bosque, Childress Creek flows into the Brazos north of Waco. Unlike the tributaries of the North Bosque, its streambed has a mostly solid limestone bottom. It does not have any big rapids, but its whitewater is continuous, dropping 20 ft/mi in its last thirteen miles. Childress offers numerous play holes and surfing spots to practice 360s. The last nine miles, from R. C. Granger Road (Bosque CR 418) to the FM 2490 bridge, is a real gem.

The four miles above Granger Road contain some surfing waves, but they are not as fun as those in the stretch below. To add a total of eight miles to the lower stretch, put in at the low-water crossing off of FM 56, upstream at Cayote.

Shredding on Childress Creek. Photo by Joey Harrell

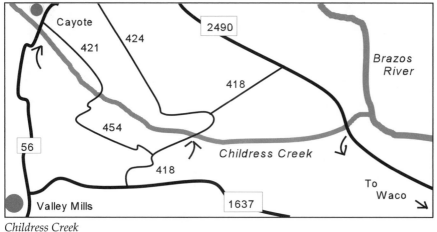

Childress Creek

Neils Creek

Run: Bosque CR 342 to SH 6		
Location: South of Clifton	County: Bosque	Drainage: 137 mi² Length: 7 miles
Gradient: 20 ft/mi Class: I–II	Gauge: North Bosque at Clifton, 2,500 cfs (6.1') minimum	

Either the North Bosque has to be really high or Cranfills Gap has to get dumped on (which occasionally does happen) for Neils Creek to be running. Like other tributaries of the North Bosque, Neils has a limestone creekbed.

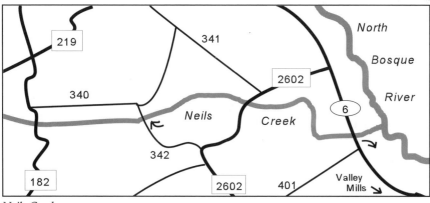

Neils Creek

Joey Harrell at the dam on Neils Creek

Despite its promising gradient, though, about all of the excitement a boater will find on this creek is a seven-foot dam about halfway through the run. A new USGS monitoring station was recently placed near the mouth of the creek. There is no easy access from either FM 182 or FM 2602.

Hog Creek

Run: Patton Church (off FM 317) to Speegleville Road		
Location: West of Waco	*County*: McLennan	*Drainage*: 78 mi² *Length*: 13 miles
Gradient: 15 ft/mi *Class*: II	*Gauge*: Hog Creek near Crawford, 3.8' minimum, 4.2' optimal	

Hog Creek is a tributary of the South Bosque which flows into Lake Waco. Its rapids are sporadic, separated by flat moving water, and in its upper parts overhanging tree limbs require maneuvering. Most of its whitewater occurs in the three miles between Shiloh Church and Onion Road. Just below Shiloh Church is the best rapid on the creek, a four-foot horseshoe-shaped drop. Bad hydraulics require portages at the dam upstream from the bridge near Compton Church and at the dam one-quarter mile upstream from Speegleville Road. At high water (seven feet) a wonderful surfing wave appears at the Shiloh Church crossing.

Several road crossings allow this run to be broken up: from Patton Church to Compton Church (three miles, 13 ft/mi), Compton Church to Compton School (two miles, 14 ft/mi), Compton School to Shiloh Church above Ocee (two miles, 15 ft/mi), Shiloh Church to Onion Road near Highland (three miles, 17 ft/mi), and Onion Road to Speegleville Road (three miles, 16 ft/mi).

Middle Bosque River

Run: Crawford (SH 317) to FM 3047		
Location: West of Waco	County: McLennan	Drainage: 182 mi² Length: 7 miles
Gradient: 13 ft/mi Class: II–III	Gauge: Middle Bosque at McGregor, 3.8' minimum, 6' high	

The Middle Bosque's drainage, limestone ledges, and scenery make it one of the state's best whitewater streams. A tributary of the South Bosque, the Middle Bosque has no rapids in the ten miles from Mosheim to Crawford. But

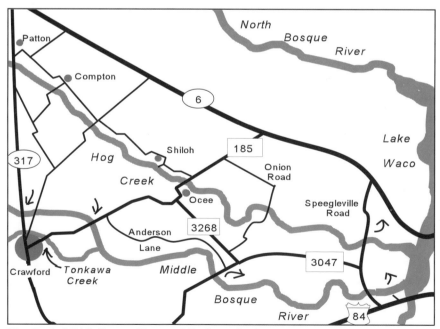

Hog Creek, Middle Bosque River, and Tonkawa Creek

Randy Barnes and Joey Harrell at the Middle Bosque's grabby hole

between SH 317 and FM 3047 (especially downstream from a good put-in at FM 185), numerous ledge combinations create opportunities for surfing and squirting. At high water, the holes and waves simply get bigger.

The four-mile section from FM 185 to FM 3047 is the most commonly run stretch. A grabby hole one mile past FM 185 (just past the confluence of Tonkawa Creek) gets mean at high water; skirt it on the right. The best play spot on the river is one-quarter mile above the takeout: a sloping slide with a good surfing wave midway down the rapid and a good side-surf hole at the bottom.

The eight miles of the Middle Bosque from FM 3047 to the Corps of Engineers landing on Lake Waco offer more surfing holes and an eight-foot dam that can be run (with speed) in the middle or off the point on river right. The run ends with more than a mile of slow-moving, flat water.

Tonkawa Creek

Run: Tonkawa Falls		
Location: Crawford, West of Waco	*County*: McLennan	*Drainage*: 30 mi² *Length*: 100 yards
Gradient: Drops 15' total *Class*: III	*Gauge*: Middle Bosque at McGregor, 4.2' minimum	

Tonkawa Falls. Photo by Tony Cooper

Tonkawa Creek joins the Middle Bosque a mile downstream from FM 185. If the Middle Bosque is at a moderate level, Tonkawa Falls (in Crawford on FM 185) is a great photo-op before you jump on the Middle Bosque. After you run the falls, stay wet and throw your boat back on your vehicle for the quick ride over to the Middle Bosque put-in only a mile away.

To run the falls, put in upstream just west of the bridge and take out on river left behind the bluff where spectators gather in the small park. Continuing down the Tonkawa to its confluence with the Middle Bosque is generally not much fun because it requires clawing through thickets of small trees in swift-moving water and bouncing over rock jumbles created by quarry debris.

Cowhouse Creek

Run: Slab Crossing to US 84		
Location: South of Hamilton	*Counties*: Hamilton, Coryell	*Drainage*: 250 mi² *Length*: 9 miles
Gradient: 18 ft/mi *Class*: II+	*Gauge*: Cowhouse Creek at Pidcoke, 1,750 cfs (7')–4,600 cfs (11')	

Above where it flows through Fort Hood into Lake Belton, Cowhouse Creek has more than thirty miles of limestone creekbeds and gravel bottoms that create rapids, occasional drops up to four feet high, and surfing play spots. The highest gradient (18 ft/mi) is in the nine miles from Slab Crossing on CR 434 (a mile south of Ohio) to US 84. To add four miles to this stretch, put in at Parsley Crossing (CR 415) upstream from Ohio between FM 1241 and US 281. Between US 84 and King (twelve miles), and King and Pidcoke (eight miles), drops and rapids are less constant but are nonetheless fun.

Barbed-wire fences stretch across the creek at most road crossings (e.g., FM 183 and CR 137, three miles upstream from King). They indicate nothing about the legality of being on the creek, but they do require deft maneuvering for you to slide under or through in moving water.

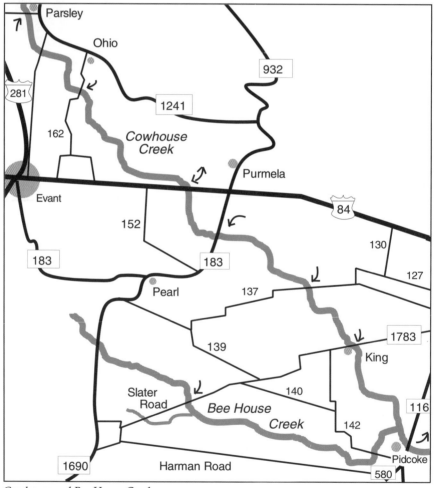

Cowhouse and Bee House Creeks

Remains of old bridge at Slab Crossing on Cowhouse Creek

Because the flow from Bee House Creek can affect the Pidcoke gauge reading, you should compare flows on the Leon River at Hamilton and Gatesville and on the Lampasas River at Kempner to make sure adequate rain fell in the upper Cowhouse drainage.

Bee House Creek

Run: Slater Road to Pidcoke		
Location: West of Fort Hood	*County*: Coryell	*Drainage*: 90 mi² *Length*: 9 miles
Gradient: 20 ft/mi *Class*: II	*Gauge*: Cowhouse Creek at Pidcoke, 2,750 cfs (8.5')–5,250 cfs (12')	

Scenic bluffs, a limestone and gravel bottom, and a continuous incline make Bee House Creek a fun run for anyone lucky enough to catch it. At low to moderate flows, its rapids are bouncy and provide intermediate paddlers practice in eddy hopping and surfing small waves. Because the gradient is continuous, many of the rapids wash out in high water. A five-foot dam three miles downstream from the put-in can be run slightly right of center or far left.

Bill Leon surfs on Bee House Creek

Low-water crossings create some hydraulics that should be punched with some momentum. At high water there is a good surfing wave-hole at a low-water crossing one-half mile upstream from the Cowhouse Creek confluence and an ender spot on Cowhouse just above the takeout bridge at Pidcoke.

Although there may not seem to be much water at the put-in (a small wooden bridge on the creek's North Fork), the South Fork adds one-third more flow 1½ miles downstream. At moderate levels, water from the South Fork will be going over the Slater Road crossing. The shuttle on the north side of the creek is five miles shorter than the one on Harman Road, but that cuts off the last 1½ miles of the creek (where there is the most continuous drop in gradient). Besides, if it is possible to cross to the north side of the creek on CR 142 one mile west of Pidcoke, then the creek is probably too low to run.

As with other creek runs in the area, special care must be taken regarding barbed-wire fences across the creek. The best time to run the creek is after heavy rains, when the fences are often washed away.

Lampasas River

Run: FM 1690 to Rumley (FM 580)		
Location: North of Lampasas	*County*: Lampasas	*Drainage*: 500 mi² *Length*: 5 miles
Gradient: 10 ft/mi *Class*: II+	*Gauge*: Lampasas River at Kempner, 900 cfs (5.5') minimum	

The large drainage of the Lampasas River makes it runnable even when other streams in the area are not. It has no technical rapids, but downstream from the School Creek confluence the Lampasas has several runnable ledges,

Mike Smith boofs a dam on the Lampasas River. © David Abel

small dams, and occasional play spots. Below the takeout bridge at FM 580 is a riverwide dam with a terminal hydraulic. Road crossings allow this run to be broken into three separate parts, each about five or six miles long.

If the FM 1690 put-in on the Lampasas seems too tame, drive a few hundred yards south on FM 2527 and check out the eight-foot waterfall where School Creek crashes into the Lampasas just downstream from the put-in. The Lampasas is narrow where the creek comes in, so if School is in session it is hard to avoid the temptation to carry your boat up to run the falls.

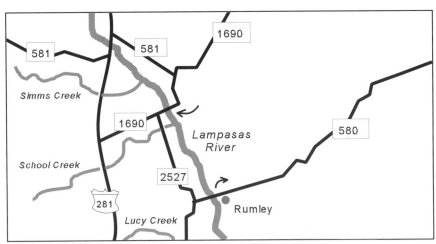

Lampasas River

Thomas Chapman drops into the Lampasas River from School Creek. © *David Abel*

Unfortunately School Creek, like its sister Lucy Creek, drains only seventy-five square miles and is too narrow upstream from FM 2527 to be considered navigable. The falls alone make it appear enticing, but that might be deceiving. The next feeder creek upstream, Simms Creek, is larger and has an eight-mile stretch west of US 281 with entertaining play spots. There is nothing on Simms east of US 281 that justifies paddling 2½ miles down to the Lampasas.

Rocky Creek

Run: US 183 to Oakalla		
Location: Southwest of Fort Hood	*County*: Burnet	*Drainage*: 115 mi² *Length*: 7½ miles
Gradient: 18 ft/mi *Class*: II	*Gauge*: South Fork of Rocky Creek near Briggs, 125 cfs (2.8') minimum	

Rocky Creek has suffered the fate of most Texas whitewater streams: it is full of dangerous dams and barbed-wire fences. Its five-foot-high, mushroom-shaped rock formations and limestone creekbed would make the creek a natural destination for paddlers were it not for these obstacles.

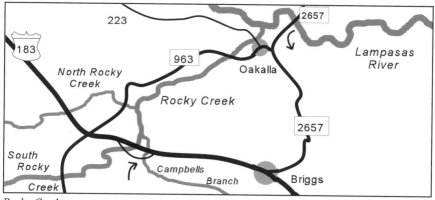

Rocky Creek

Downstream from the put-in on Campbell's Branch, South Rocky Creek provides much of the creek's flow. North Rocky Creek adds more volume 1½ miles downstream. Just as the rock formations begin to make the run look interesting, the first of the six dams and six fences appears. Some of the dams can be run at low water, but they are very dangerous at levels that would make this a fun play run.

Past the FM 963 takeout at Oakalla, the creek continues for another mile before it joins the Lampasas. It is two more miles from there to a better take-out on FM 2657.

One of the minicanyons of limestone on Rocky Creek

Salado Creek

Run: FM 2843 to Salado		
Location: Southwest of Temple	County: Bell	Drainage: 137 mi² Length: 5 miles
Gradient: 12 ft/mi Class: II+		Gauge: Berry Creek at Weir, 400 cfs (4') minimum

Not to be confused with the creek of the same name near San Antonio, Salado Creek is a scenic, limestone-bottomed stream that cuts through the escarpment of the Edwards Plateau and ends amid the quaint shops and restaurants of the former stagecoach town of Salado. At high water the creek has good play spots and several moderately technical drops that require good boat control. A heavy sweep-away chain-link fence a mile from the put-in and another in the middle of a boulder drop make high-water runs interesting.

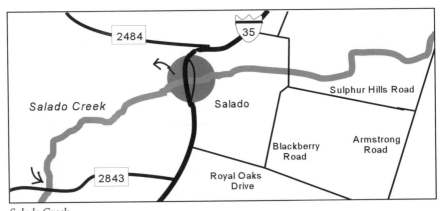

Salado Creek

Berry Creek

Run: I-35 to FM 971 (Weir)		
Location: North of Georgetown	County: Williamson	Drainage: 127 mi² Length: 4 miles
Gradient: 11 ft/mi Class: II		Gauge: Berry Creek at Weir, 400 cfs (4') minimum

This run has several small ledge drops and short rapids, along with an occasional dam. An alternate put-in is four miles upstream at Shell Road. If you put in on FM 971, you can float a mile on Berry Creek to its confluence with the San Gabriel River to run the four-mile stretch that provides surfing opportunities above the SH 29 crossing. To make a ten-mile day run, combine the small-creek feel of the last four miles of Berry Creek with the lower half of the San Gabriel run. If the combined flow of Berry and the San Gabriel is above 3,000 cfs, the nice surfing possibilities on the San Gabriel disappear.

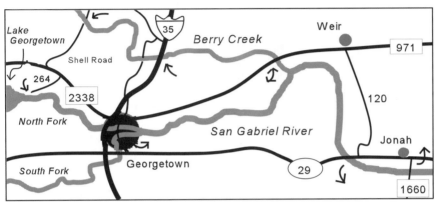

Berry Creek and San Gabriel River (including North Fork below Lake Georgetown)

San Gabriel River (below Georgetown)

Run: Georgetown City Park to SH 29		
Location: Georgetown	County: Williamson	Drainage: 405 mi² Length: 7 miles
Gradient: 10 ft/mi Class: II+	Gauge: Add Berry Creek and the North and South Forks of the San Gabriel, 1,600–3,000 cfs total	

The release from Lake Georgetown on the North Fork of the San Gabriel and the natural flow of the South Fork can combine to supply enough water to make the San Gabriel River below Georgetown a delight. Two city parks in Georgetown provide put-in options. The first park is on the South Fork in town just to the east of I-35. The second park, where there is a marginally runnable dam and a low-water crossing, is on the north side of the river downstream from the confluence of the forks.

Although there are some play spots in the first half of the run, better surfing, slants, and holes are scattered over a 1½-mile stretch below where

Berry Creek comes in, about a mile above the takeout. Because of that, some boaters prefer to put in on Berry Creek. For a longer run with more play spots, take out in Jonah, three miles downstream from SH 29 at FM 1660. The gradient for those three miles—especially the first—is slightly higher (11 ft/mi) than the upper stretch.

Flooding in 1997 and 1998 filled in some of the ledge holes and changed some of the best surfing waves into ripples. This shows how rivers are not constrained by guidebooks.

Mike Smith surfs a wave on the main San Gabriel below Georgetown. © David Abel

San Gabriel River, North Fork (below Lake Georgetown)

Run: Lake Georgetown Dam to Georgetown City Park		
Location: Georgetown	*County*: Williamson	*Drainage*: 268 mi² *Length*: 4 miles
Gradient: 13 ft/mi *Class*: II	*Gauge*: North Fork of San Gabriel River at Georgetown, 250 cfs (6.3') minimum	

Because it depends on releases from Lake Georgetown, this little stretch is sometimes runnable even when everything else is too low. It has some small surfing waves, good stern-squirt eddy lines, and a challenging rapid (called Sonic because of the nearby burger haunt) downstream of the I-35 bridge. Before that, midway through the run, a five-foot dam can be run at medium levels far left and at low water just about anywhere; portage on the right. Because of its accessibility and ease, the North Fork is a good training stream.

To get to the put-in at the base of the dam, turn off FM 2328 onto CR 264 (Lakeway Drive or Booty's Crossing Road). For dam release information, consult Today's Reservoir Report at the Corps of Engineers Web site (http:// swf66-wc.usace.army.mil).

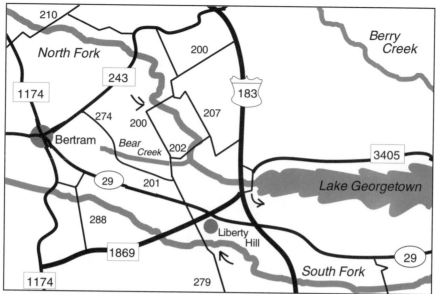

Upper North Fork and South Fork of the San Gabriel River

San Gabriel River, North Fork (above Lake Georgetown)

Run: CR 200 (Mount Horeb) to US 183		
Location: West of Georgetown	*County*: Williamson	*Drainage*: 247 mi² *Length*: 8 miles
Gradient: 12 ft/mi *Class*: II–III	*Gauge*: South Fork of San Gabriel River at Georgetown, 400 cfs (4.7') minimum	

Because of the size of its drainage area, the North Fork of the San Gabriel is run more often than many other nearby streams. At high water it sports a bunch of play spots and surfing waves and even throws in occasional holes to punch. Fast surfing waves are especially abundant downstream of the CR 202 crossing at mile 4. The most popular surfing hole is just downstream of the US 183 crossing near the takeout.

It is not unusual to find groups of paddlers from Austin on the river when it is up. For years there was no whitewater stream in the immediate area other than Barton Creek that was more popular than the North Fork of the San Gabriel. The fact that other creeks are now becoming more well-known has not prevented paddlers from returning to the North Fork to enjoy its treasures. If the river is really high, check out the many waves and holes on Bear Creek.

Kirk Beckendorf surfs a hole on the North Fork of the San Gabriel above Lake Georgetown.
© *David Abel*

San Gabriel River, South Fork

Run: Liberty Hill to Georgetown		
Location: West of Georgetown	*County*: Williamson	*Drainage*: 133 mi² *Length*: 18 miles
Gradient: 14 ft/mi *Class*: II		*Gauge*: South Fork of San Gabriel, 300 cfs (4.5') minimum

Two miles southeast of Liberty Hill (CR 279) the South Fork of the San Gabriel begins a 15 ft/mi drop for five miles to US 183. Scenic limestone bluffs overlook the river near the put-in just below the old Martha Chapman Dam. Although the South Fork has more overall gradient than the North Fork, it attracts fewer play boaters. Still, surfing spots pop up frequently enough to make the run interesting for groups with a mixture of skill levels.

From US 183 to its confluence with the North Fork in Georgetown, the South Fork cruises along at about 14 ft/mi in a wide streambed that has occasional play spots. Less than a mile downstream from US 183, the river courses through some boulders over a gently sloping ledge. CR 267 crosses the river shortly thereafter. Two miles downstream is a second low-water crossing (CR

268). Be careful passing under the two sweep-away fences that stretch across the river about four miles upstream from Georgetown. Take out either at the park in Georgetown before the North Fork confluence (just to the east of I-35) or after the confluence at City Park.

Brushy Creek

Run: FM 620 to Forest Creek Golf Club Road (CR 122)		
Location: Round Rock	County: Williamson	Drainage: 80 mi²
		Length: 6 miles
Gradient: 14 ft/mi Class: II+	Gauge: South Fork of San Gabriel, 400 cfs (4.7'); Berry Creek, 375 (3.9'); and Bull Creek, 100 cfs (3.5') minimum	

A secret favorite of some Austin boaters, Brushy Creek is a tree-covered stream that flows through Round Rock when heavy rains fall around Cedar Park and north Austin. It is formed when its two forks come together just to the west of town, and it runs along CR 174 (Harry Mann Road) in the mostly flat upper two miles.

The best put-in is behind the businesses on FM 620 upstream from Chisholm Trail Road just west of I-35. The four-foot dam at the put-in can be run on the far left. After the creek goes under I-35, it flows through Round Rock Memorial Park. Another mile downstream a second city park signals a ten-foot dam (which can be run with momentum in the middle).

Scenic bluffs and small rapids pepper the rest of the run. Surf spots occur in the last mile where the creekbed is limestone. Take out at the low-water

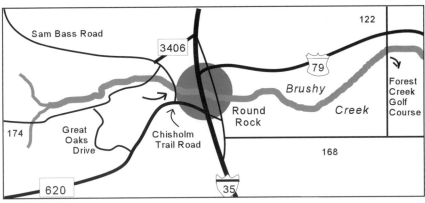

Brushy Creek

Steve Mills runs the dam on Brushy Creek

crossing downstream from Forest Creek Golf Club Road (CR 122) south of US 79, just around the bend from the last play spot.

Lagniappe: The historic "round rock" is a ten-foot round limestone platform that protrudes above water level (except at high flows); it is immediately downstream from the Chisholm Trail Road crossing. For those hooked on the Mexican food at Herbert's near the Rio Vista Dam on the San Marcos River, El Matador in downtown Round Rock is a must-stop.

Brazos River at Port Sullivan

Run: Play spots north of FM 485		
Location: West of Hearne	County: Milam	Drainage: 21,000 mi² Length: 1½ miles
Gradient: 5 ft/mi Class: I–II	Gauge: Brazos River at SH 21 near Bryan, 11–18'	

South of Waco the Brazos is generally a wide and slow-moving river. At Marlin's Falls-on-the-Brazos Park are a couple of two-foot ledges that give Falls County its name. Other than those two small surfing spots, there is no whitewater on the Brazos until Port Sullivan, where the river cuts through sandstone composite outcroppings in the riverbed west of Hearne. When Robertson, Milam, and Falls Counties get rain, or when Lake Whitney and Lake Waco are releasing, these outcroppings create rapids.

The two rapids at Port Sullivan are good places for beginners to practice eddy turns, peel-outs, and ferrying, but don't expect much in terms of surfing at low-water levels. At moderate levels there are some challenging attainment moves and small surfing spots, especially at the second rapid, visible upstream from the FM 485 bridge. The first rapid, which is out of sight of the bridge, is a good place to practice eddy hopping.

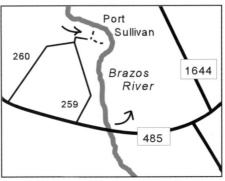

Brazos River at Port Sullivan

The put-in is one-quarter mile above the picnic and camping area overlooking the first rapid. The overlook and put-in are accessible through a pasture just to the east of the Port Sullivan cemetery. The pasture owner charges a fee of $2 per person at the gate. To avoid the shuttle and the fee, at low water some boaters simply paddle upstream from the FM 485 bridge to the two rapids.

Lagniappe: In the 1850s Port Sullivan was a thriving steamboat port, with its own college and several thousand residents. When the railroad bypassed it, most of its buildings were dismantled and moved eight miles east to Hearne. Today the overgrown cemetery with some fancy grave markers is the only remnant of the town's past glory.

Brazos River at Hidalgo Falls

Run: Play spot west of FM 159		
Location: West of Navasota	*County:* Brazos	*Drainage:* 31,566 mi² *Length:* ¼ mile
Gradient: Drops about 8' *Class:* II–II+	*Gauge:* Brazos River at SH 21 near Bryan, 11–22'	

During low-water periods, boaters in Southeast Texas grow desperate and any water that splashes looks pretty good. On weekends when Hidalgo Falls is running, paddlers from Houston, College Station, Austin, and Waco show up. Occasionally, even some poor souls from Dallas and Louisiana drive four

or five hours just to play there. Small shops in Navasota (eight minutes away) can entertain those who want to get out of the heat or who forget to bring something to read while the hole-hogs work on their 360s.

Hidalgo Falls is the place to be when dams upstream on the Brazos, San Gabriel, Leon, and Lampasas Rivers are releasing. Here the Brazos is a hundred yards wide and the falls are a series of drops over composite sandstone ledges, bore holes, and islands. At low levels (eleven feet) Hidalgo has some eddy lines for squirting, a couple of side-surfing holes, and small surfing waves. At fourteen feet some four-foot waves create fast surfing, and at eighteen feet good ender spots appear. Above nineteen feet

Randy Barnes does a pirouette at Hidalgo Falls on the Brazos. © David Abel

retendos and dynamic surfing are the norm. And above twenty-three feet the whole thing washes out.

Every year or so a combination of heat, drinking, and lack of life vests results in someone drowning in Hidalgo's swirling currents. At high water it

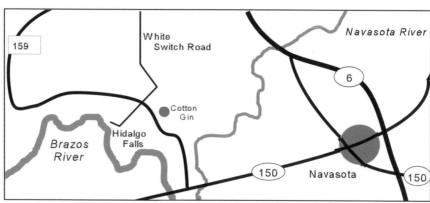

Hidalgo Falls on the Brazos River

is no place to swim: undercuts and fierce turbulence along some eddy lines test the best of
paddlers. When they fail to roll, boaters sometimes end up chasing after their gear in swift
current for up to a quarter mile. When that
happens, especially during winter months,
swimmers feel the embrace of *los brazos de
Dios*, the arms of God.

If you use the Hempstead gauge, subtract
three feet plus anything coming in from the
Navasota River. If heavy rain south of Bryan
has caused the Navasota to rise appreciably,
then rely more on the Bryan gauge. Additional
flow is contributed by Yegua Creek, due to
releases from Lake Somerville. For release
rates, consult Today's Reservoir Report at the
Corps of Engineers Web site (http://swf66.swf-
wc.usace.army.mil).

To get to Hidalgo from Navasota, go west
on SH 105 3.5 miles, turn north on FM 159,
and go 3.2 miles (past the cotton gin on the
right). Turn left into the cornfield on the gravel
road that crosses FM 159 (the right turn heads
over the railroad tracks on White Switch Road)
and drive to the end. Usually Tannie is there to
collect a fee ($1 per car) for access to the river,
but if he isn't, put the money in the box
provided. To the left is an overlook where you
can scope out the whole rapid from high on the
bluff. To the right (upriver 100 yards near two
abandoned camp houses) is the Slide, a thirty-
foot zoom flume into the river that is guaran-
teed to get your blood pumping. Most paddlers
park in a clearing near the money box between
the overlook and the Slide. A path going down
to the river through a bamboo stand is the
easiest access route. Camping is available ($5
per car); there are bathrooms and faucets but no
showers.

When Hidalgo Falls is too low, boaters
from Houston sometimes find moving water
ninety-two miles downstream on the Brazos

*Going for retentive moves at
Hidalgo Falls. Photos by David
Abel*

The Slide at Hidalgo Falls. © David Abel

south of Stephen F. Austin State Park. About a mile below FM 1458 in San Felipe, the river drops over a small ledge fancifully named Killer Fang Falls. At moderate levels, the drop disappears and the run from FM 1458 to I-10 becomes a five-mile float trip.

PART FOUR

~

Colorado River Drainage

Thirteen-year-old Kyle Scarbrough submerges at Twin Falls on Barton Creek. © *David Abel*

Colorado River Drainage

THE COLORADO RIVER BASIN extends eighty miles into New Mexico, but the river actually begins its 865-mile trek to the Gulf of Mexico in Dawson County in West Texas. It meanders through prairieland, gets backed up in reservoirs, and picks up flow from the Concho and San Saba Rivers before it reaches the Hill Country in San Saba County. Dams in the Hill Country have tamed the river, although place names like Marble Falls recall the days when the river must have been a whitewater dream.

Today rapids are limited mostly to the tributaries of the Colorado. There are some play spots on the main river (e.g., in the outflows of Austin-area dams), but most talk of whitewater in the Colorado drainage involves either the technical challenges of creeks near Austin (e.g., Barton Creek) or the big-water (20,000+ cfs) features of the Llano and Pedernales Rivers.

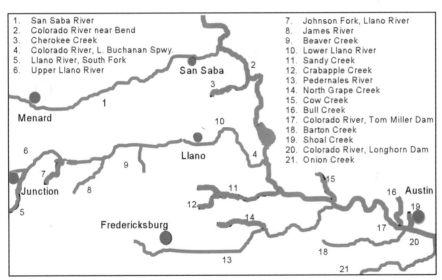

1. San Saba River
2. Colorado River near Bend
3. Cherokee Creek
4. Colorado River, L. Buchanan Spwy.
5. Llano River, South Fork
6. Upper Llano River
7. Johnson Fork, Llano River
8. James River
9. Beaver Creek
10. Lower Llano River
11. Sandy Creek
12. Crabapple Creek
13. Pedernales River
14. North Grape Creek
15. Cow Creek
16. Bull Creek
17. Colorado River, Tom Miller Dam
18. Barton Creek
19. Shoal Creek
20. Colorado River, Longhorn Dam
21. Onion Creek

Colorado River whitewater tributaries

Recently paddlers have discovered that the creeks that feed into the larger streams are as exciting and challenging as the Colorado, Pedernales, and Llano Rivers. Because some of these creeks cut through granite, schist, and gneiss rock formations instead of the typical Hill Country limestone, they have characteristics more like whitewater runs in New Mexico and Colorado. Unlike their western counterparts, though, these creeks are not supplied with flow from snowmelt. They are therefore runnable only after infrequent downpours.

San Saba River

Run: FM 1311 to FM 2732		
Location: Southwest of San Saba	Counties: Mason, McCulloch, San Saba	Drainage: 1,200 mi² Length: 40 miles
Gradient: 10 ft/mi Class: II+	Gauges: San Saba at Menard (LCRA), 400 cfs (3.45') minimum; at Brady, 500 cfs (3.7'); at San Saba, 900 cfs (6.3')	

The San Saba River flows clear and clean for about 100 miles through mostly undeveloped ranch land north of Mason. During high-water periods, its occasional ledges create grabby holes and surfing waves comparable to those on other Edwards Plateau rivers. As with the Llano River, there is also a lot of flat water.

The best stretches with the most interesting drops are those with the steepest gradient, especially near Voca Crossing. Paddlers can select short stretches or combine any of these options:

- FM 1311 to US 377, fifteen miles at 10 ft/mi (one mile at 20 ft/mi)
- US 377 to SH 71 (Voca), three miles at 18 ft/mi
- SH 71 (Voca) to FM 1851, one mile at 10 ft/mi
- FM 1851 to McCulloch CR 212, five miles at 7 ft/mi
- McCulloch CR 212 to San Saba CR 233 (extension of FM 2732), sixteen miles at 10 ft/mi

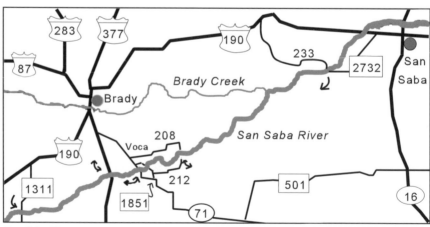

San Saba River

The best long day run is the nineteen-mile stretch from FM 1311 to FM 1851, and the most remote run is the last sixteen miles through a scenic canyon.

In addition to the LCRA gauge at San Saba, there are San Saba River gauges at Menard and south of Brady. The Brady gauge is especially helpful for runs near Voca.

Lagniappe: Reconstructed remains of San Saba Presidio, an eighteenth-century Spanish fort, are a mile upstream from Menard.

Colorado River near Bend

Run: Bend to Colorado Bend State Recreation Area (Lemon Springs)		
Location: West of Lampasas	*Counties*: Lampasas, San Saba	*Drainage*: 31,500 mi²
		Length: 16 miles
Gradient: 3 ft/mi *Class*: I–II	*Gauge*: Colorado River at Red Bluff (LCRA), 500 cfs (3.1') minimum	

Four shoal-like rapids offer minimal surfing opportunities on this stretch of the Colorado, but high limestone bluffs make it a scenic day trip or pleasant overnighter. If the river is high, more challenging things are probably

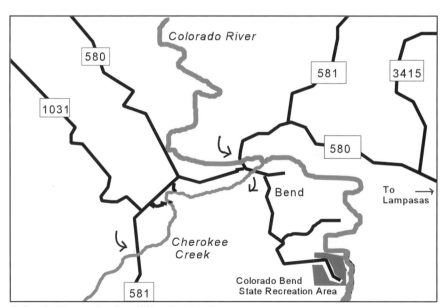

Colorado River at Bend and Cherokee Creek

happening in the area. Gorman Falls is a seventy-five-foot incline of travertine and ferns that spills into the river at mile 12.

Put in from the flat rock area upstream from the FM 580 crossing. The easiest camping for an overnight trip is at two fishing camps on the west side of the river, where you can park vehicles before putting on the river. For more privacy you have to go downriver a bit farther; be sure, however, that you do not set up camp on private property without permission. Just camp in the riverbed or no more than halfway between the top and bottom of the riverbank. Take out at Colorado Bend State Recreation Area.

On the USGS gauge list, the LCRA site is identified as the Colorado River near San Saba.

Cherokee Creek

Run: High Valley Church to Colorado Bend SRA Road		
Location: West of Lampasas	County: San Saba	Drainage: 160 mi² Length: 9 miles
Gradient: 23 ft/mi Class: III–IV		Gauge: Cherokee Creek at FM 501 (LCRA), 5.5' minimum

With the exception of Crabapple Creek, Cherokee Creek is probably the best whitewater creek in the state. It is an almost nonstop playground of waves, holes, pourovers, and whirlpools. The scenery is great, wildlife such as beaver abound, access is easy, and the shuttle is quick. It is destined to become one of the all-time favorites of whitewater paddlers.

Cherokee Creek enters the Colorado River just downstream from the flat rock put-in of the Colorado Bend stretch. If the road going to Colorado Bend State Recreation Area from Bend is covered, there is enough water to paddle Cherokee. FM 501 parallels the creek, and alternate access points occur at crossings on the High Valley Church Road four and five miles downstream from the put-in.

To avoid hassles with the landowner on the northeast side of the put-in bridge, park your vehicle on the south side of the creek. Between the bridge support and a barbed-wire fence, squeeze through the narrow slot to access the creek under the bridge. Things are mellow for approximately the first mile; then it seems that you are never out of sight or sound of rapids and play spots. About a mile below the second Valley Church Road crossing, the creek crashes over a seven-foot ledge that can be run on the far right. Downstream the waves and holes just keep coming at you. In a word, bliss.

Jimmy Vick at the big ledge on Cherokee Creek

Colorado River (Lake Buchanan Spillway)

Run: Lake Buchanan Dam to SH 29		
Location: West of Burnet	*County*: Burnet	*Drainage*: 20,512 mi² *Length*: 1 mile
Gradient: 120 ft/mi *Class*: V		*Gauge*: Use LCRA information about water going over the dam

Every few years very heavy rains cause Lake Buchanan (between Burnet and Llano) to rise to levels that require the LCRA to divert water over the spillway. The one-mile cascade created by the diversion is something to behold. Even if it does not have the intensity of some hair runs elsewhere in the United States, its pinning possibilities and pourovers make it one of the most intimidating stretches of whitewater in Texas.

As elsewhere, before you run a stretch like the Buchanan Spillway, scout it thoroughly when no water is being released; then run it in short segments, taking every precaution. Unfortunately, that requires patience, years of waiting, and the ability to take advantage of the few days when water is released.

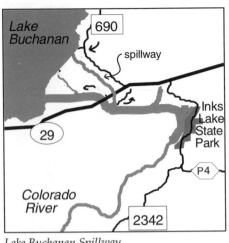

Lake Buchanan Spillway

Those who have run it tell tales of lost boats and other forms of carnage. To capture the beauty of this run, don't forget the video camera.

The trail from the parking lot at the dam to the beginning of the spillway is fenced off, so you have to access the run by carrying your boat upstream from the river. That torturous hike provides numerous opportunities to scout the drops.

For information about the lake level and dam release schedule, see the LCRA Web site or the Corps of Engineers site (http://swf66. swf-wc.usace.army.mil).

South Fork of the Llano River

Run: Telegraph to South Llano River SP		
Location: South of Junction	*County*: Kimble	*Drainage*: 748 mi² *Length*: 10 miles
Gradient: 12 ft/mi *Class*: I–II	*Gauge*: Llano at Junction, 400 cfs (1.4') minimum	

Most paddlers know of the South Fork of the Llano River from its reputation as a pleasant warm weather float trip. It is fed by hundreds of springs in the area, so for much of the year its clean, clear water creates small rapids, especially near the first US 377 crossing south of Junction. From the second US 377 crossing (just north of Telegraph) to the bridges at Boone and Greene Crossings, there are a few ledge drops where the channel narrows and forms eddy lines where beginners can practice ferrying and eddy turns.

During high water, most drops wash out. When that happens, a two-foot falls downstream of the first US 377 crossing becomes a good surf spot.

If the rain has fallen west and north of Junction, then the gauge reading reflects flow from the North Fork rather than the South Fork. The North Fork is smaller than its counterpart and has fewer rapids. Because it also has less gradient and is impounded by several dams, it hardly matches the charm of the South Fork.

Lagniappe: According to the Texas State Travel Guide, Kimble County has more flowing streams than any other county in the state. Of course, that does not mean that Junction is the state's whitewater capital, but it does mean that there might be runs in the area that are waiting to be discovered in those normally arid hills.

The Llano does not get high in Junction without large amounts of water cascading down potentially interesting creekbeds. To find out exactly where the water is rising, check flash flood warnings, road closings, and radar reports.

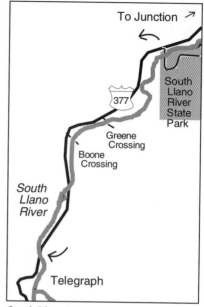

South Llano River

Upper Llano River

Run: Kimble CR 310 to Kimble CR 314		
Location: East of Junction	*County*: Kimble	*Drainage*: 1,849 mi² *Length*: 12 miles
Gradient: 7 ft/mi *Class*: I–II	*Gauge*: Llano River at Junction, 750 cfs (2.3') minimum	

From where its North and South Forks come together in Junction, the Llano River flows through mostly remote ranch land for about 100 miles before joining the Colorado River at Lake LBJ. For many of those miles the river is wide and flat. But occasionally it drops over small ledges or swirls around granite and gneiss boulders to form challenging drops at high water.

There is not much whitewater in the upper stretches of the river. Five miles downstream from a put-in at the Junction City Park on the South Llano River—not far downstream from the CR 310 crossing (also known as Mason Crossing)—the Llano reaches Nethery Falls. The falls consist of a gradual incline of two or three feet over about twenty-five yards and a conglomerate

Nethery Falls on the upper Llano River. Courtesy Michael Van Winkle

ledge that runs across the entire river, which funnels some of the flow into a two-foot-high, horseshoe-shaped drop in the middle. When the river is flooding, large surfing waves appear there and in a boulder garden downstream. But since the river level drops quickly, the window for taking advantage of flooding conditions is usually no more than two days.

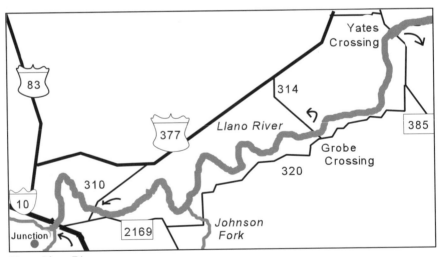
Upper Llano River

In the fifteen miles from Nethery Falls down to FM 385 (Yates Crossing) there are few rapids and only occasional surfing waves at high water. If you take out at Grobe Crossing on CR 314, you cut off five of those tedious miles of flat water.

Johnson Fork of the Llano River

Run: FM 2169 to Kimble CR 320		
Location: East of Junction	*County*: Kimble	*Drainage*: 275 mi² *Length*: 3½ miles
Gradient: 15 ft/mi *Class*: Perhaps II+		*Gauge*: Llano River at Junction, probably 2,000 cfs (4.8') minimum

If the area around Junction really gets pounded and the area north of Segovia floods, then the Johnson Fork of the Llano River might be up. This as-yet-unrun stretch begins at the third crossing of FM 2169 north of Segovia. It has a granite creekbed, so unlike the Llano's other forks its drops might be more interesting than the ledges one finds elsewhere in the Hill Country. It is also more constricted than other area streams (especially the much wider Llano), so its isolated canyon might have some really challenging drops.

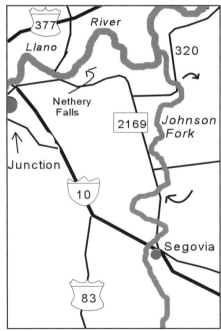

To know if the Johnson Fork is running requires either personal inspection or a creative interpretation of gauge reports. The fork flows into the Llano downstream from the gauge at Junction and upstream from the gauge at Mason. Before the Llano reaches Mason, though, the James River adds its contribution to the flow. You cannot readily discern if the increase at Mason is due to a rise on Johnson Fork or the James River. The key is to monitor road closings and the radar.

Johnson Fork of the Llano River

James River

Run: FM 385 to FM 2389		
Location: South-west of Mason	*County*: Mason	*Drainage*: 245 mi² *Length*: 18 miles
Gradient: 18 ft/mi *Class*: Perhaps II–III	*Gauge*: Llano River at Mason, perhaps more than 18,000 cfs (7.85')	

Although one would assume that the James River has been run, I cannot find anyone who has tested its scenic solitude in the high water conditions necessary to make it interesting. Once I tried to reach it after heavy rains, only to discover that the bridges I had to cross had been washed away. At other times when I could get there, the water was too low. One of these days, some-one will catch it at just the right level and discover the beauty of its solid rock creekbed and red sandstone canyon.

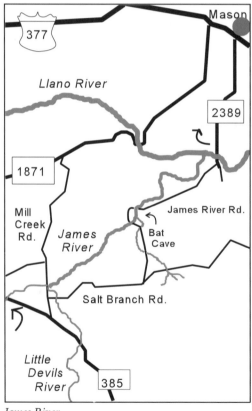

James River

If there is enough water for the James, you probably won't be able to cross the Llano on FM 385 from the north. The flow at the put-in bridge (which should be im-passable) will increase by more than half when the Little Devils River (a.k.a East Fork of the James) meets the James (a.k.a. West Fork of the Little Devils) four miles down-stream. From there the creek-bed is rock and the gradient is dependable. At the Eckert James River Bat Cave (where Salt Creek comes in) the river broadens. But four miles from the Llano, it enters a red rock canyon where the best pros-pects for technical rapids exist. The takeout is on the Llano at the FM 2389 cross-ing south of Mason.

The James should be running if the Llano at Mason is at 18,000 cfs, with less than half of that at the Llano gauge at Junction. If the flow is more than half, it is likely that the James is not contributing enough to make the run worthwhile. Crossings on the Llano on FM 385 (Yates Crossing) and FM 1871 will be impassable, so the only dependable shuttle route involves driving back through Fredericksburg to Mason (a total of eighty miles each way). At minimal levels, FM 783 should be passable (and this cuts the drive to fifty-five miles each way). Still, that's quite a shuttle for an unknown run.

Landowners and local law enforcement officials consider the riverbed private property ceded by Spanish land grants. Even when the streambed is privately owned, though, the water remains public property. To be on the safe side, however, stay in your boat.

Lagniappe: Home to six million bats, the James River Bat Cave is administered by the Nature Conservancy and is open on Friday and Saturday nights.

Beaver Creek

Run: Spring Branch Road to US 87		
Location: southeast of Mason	*County*: Mason	*Drainage*: 215 mi² *Length*: 11 miles
Gradient: 20 ft/mi *Class*: III	*Gauge*: Beaver Creek near Mason, 325 cfs (3.1') minimum	

Beaver Creek is representative of the creeks that cut through the granite of the Llano Uplift on their way to the Llano. To the north are Willow Creek, Martin Creek, Elm Creek, San Fernando Creek, and Little Llano Creek. Flowing in from the south are Beaver Creek, Hickory Creek, Sixmile Creek, and Honey Creek. All have gradients in excess of 20 ft/mi, and some get as high as 45 ft/mi. The opportunity to run them is limited to periods of torrential downpours, but because of the rock formations that comprise their creekbeds, die-hard creekers won't want to miss the chance to catch them when they are up. Besides Beaver Creek, Hickory and Sixmile Creeks have the best gradient-drainage combinations.

Beaver Creek

Joey Harrell paddles over one of the granite drops on Beaver Creek

As with the other creeks, it takes a lot of rain to get Beaver up, especially in the six-mile stretch from north of Doss to the Hilda crossing east of FM 783. Below the Loeffler Road crossing near Hilda, the creek is a combination of pools and rocky drops of polished granite. In several spots boulders constrict the current to form interesting chutes and, at high water, turbulent rapids.

Deer, wild turkeys, and barbed-wire fences are everywhere. Paddle this creek only after huge floods have taken out most of the fences, or be prepared to squeeze through or under strands of barbed wire in moving water. At high water you might be able to paddle over the fences, but such a run would be

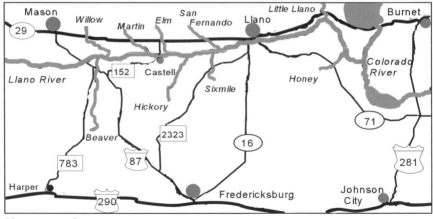

Llano area creeks

exceedingly dangerous (especially in the stretch just above and below the Simonsville Road crossing, 1½ miles downstream from Hilda).

Lower Llano River

Run: Llano to FM 3404		
Location: East of Llano	County: Llano	Drainage: 4,192 mi² Length: 19 miles
Gradient: 8 ft/mi Class: II–III (IV)	Gauge: Llano River at Mason, 3,000 cfs (5.2'); Llano River at Llano, 5,000 cfs (7') minimum	

Except for a few ledges, the twenty miles of the Llano from FM 385 to White's Crossing (FM 1871) southwest of Mason is mostly flat water. Scenic red rock bluffs appear as the Llano approaches the James River near Mason. Two miles downstream from FM 1871, Simmons Hole (a.k.a. Soldiers Crossing) provides one of the few technical spots—a class-II sharp turn around rocks and up against a wall. Two more miles downstream, FM 2389 crosses just past the James River confluence. From there to US 87, the river offers few whitewater features but flows nicely for eleven picturesque miles.

At high water, surfing rapids appear occasionally in the twelve miles from US 87 to Castell. Gneiss and granite outcroppings of the Llano Uplift form play spots in the first two miles and one class III– rapid midway in the run. More ledges in the five miles from Castell to CR 103 form monster holes and waves. Here the river is more than 100 yards wide, so a swim would be epic.

The big water run on the Llano begins at the Llano city park west of SH 16 and ends at FM 3404 just before Lake LBJ. When the flow is greater than 10,000 cfs (nine feet) on the Llano gauge, several large slanting drops up to ten feet high create Grand Canyon-sized waves and holes. The largest drop

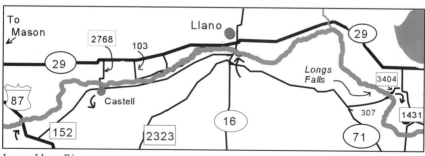

Lower Llano River

(Longs Falls), two miles upstream from the takeout, is easily accessed at Longs Fishing Camp off of FM 1431 north of Kingsland. A small sign usually adorned with catfish heads points to the fishing camp; entrance costs $5 per person. At high water small play spots form across the Slab, a large rock area where the FM 3404 low-water bridge crosses the river near Kingsland.

Sandy Creek

Run: Llano CR 310 to SH 71		
Location: Southeast of Llano	County: Llano	Drainage: 299 mi²
		Length: 4 miles
Gradient: 21 ft/mi	Gauge: Sandy Creek at SH 71, 500	
Class: II+	cfs (6.2') minimum	

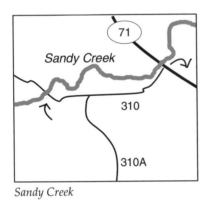

Sandy Creek

Although Sandy Creek cuts through a ridge with several named mountains, any rapids that once might have existed in the folds of granite upstream from the put-in have since filled with sand.

Two rapids near the put-in are interesting at high water, though. The first is a series of broken ledges; the second is an extended drop through granite boulders. Combined, they offer a couple of hours of technical paddling diversion.

Crabapple Creek

Run: Eckert Road to RM 965		
Location: North of Fredericksburg	County: Gillespie	Drainage: 93 mi²
		Length: 8 miles
Gradient: 52 ft/mi; 1 mi at 100 ft/mi, 1 mi at 70 ft/mi	Gauge: Pedernales River at Fredericksburg, 1,500 cfs (8.7'); or Sandy Creek at	
Class: IV	SH 71, 2,000+ cfs (7.4')	

At 20 cfs Crabapple Creek looks deceptively placid before starting to drop up to 100 ft/mi

Crabapple Creek is the closest thing to steep creek paddling you'll find in Texas. It is without question the best whitewater creek in the state. Even with its small drainage, Crabapple comes up relatively often. If you are lucky enough to be able to run it, you'll think you died and went to Colorado.

Nowhere else in the Lone Star State will you find a creek with its 100 ft/mi gradient and technical challenge. Landowners don't like the thought that the creek meets the statutory definition of navigability, so until someone gets the matter decided in court, expect some hassles.

Beginning at its headwaters between Fredericksburg and Enchanted Rock State Park, Crabapple Creek flows twenty miles before dropping into a gorge carved down through the granite of the Llano Uplift. At the head of the gorge is

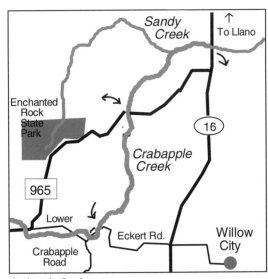

Crabapple Creek

a fifteen-foot-high dam that can be portaged on the right. From there on down it is one slot move or boof after another. Several spots deserve scouting, and one in particular (an undercut bank shot) might require a carry. Blown-away remnants of barbed-wire fences pop up periodically in the last two miles.

The as-yet unrun five miles from the take-out to where Crabapple joins Sandy Creek drop about 20 ft/mi. At FM 965 Crabapple is at least 150 feet wide and probably has interesting rapids downstream if granite outcroppings constrict the channel. From the Crabapple Creek confluence to the SH 16 crossing a mile downstream, Sandy Creek is wide and drops 10 ft/mi.

Lagniappe: Fredericksburg is well known for its shops, bed and breakfast inns, German cuisine, and historical sites such as the Admiral Nimitz Museum. For rock climbers and hikers, there is hardly a nicer spot than the 500-foot-high granite Enchanted Rock. During rainy periods in the winter (when Crabapple would be more likely to run) the state park might be closed to the public for hunters seeking Bambi's mother.

Pedernales River

Run: FM 1 (West of Hye) to Johnson City (US 281)		
Location: West of Johnson City	*County*: Blanco	*Drainage*: 901 mi² *Length*: 16 miles
Gradient: 17 ft/mi *Class*: II–III; high water, III–IV–	*Gauge*: Pedernales at Fredericksburg, 700 cfs (6.8'); at Johnson City, low 1,500 cfs (11.3'); moderate 8,000 cfs (13'), high 15,000 cfs (14.5')	

The granite ledges and shoals of this increasingly popular run provide some of the biggest waves and holes in the state. After heavy rain, flows of 40,000 cfs or more crash over drops up to eight feet high, creating scary hydraulics and wonderful surfing opportunities. Because the river is often more than 100 yards wide, a swim at moderate to high levels could be dangerous, so a combat roll is essential.

In its westernmost reaches near Fredericksburg, the Pedernales River does not have as much gradient as farther downstream near Johnson City. In recent years paddlers have generally preferred the stretch from Sandy Crossing (FM 1320) to Johnson City. But because there are some interesting drops upstream, I have included another 3½ miles in my suggested run. Sixteen miles may seem long, but at high water you move along between three and four miles per hour.

Between the put-in at the roadside park west of Hye and the big falls are two five-foot drops with grabby holes at higher water. The eight-foot falls are the worst far left, rockiest far right, and the cleanest left of center. Boat scouting is risky, but because the river is so wide there, scouting from the bank is almost useless. Great surfing holes abound between the falls and the Sandy Crossing bridge.

In the 12½ miles from the Sandy Crossing bridge to Johnson City, the granite is replaced by shale and limestone. There are nine nice rapids (each a few hundred yards long). Five of these play stretches (and a runnable dam) occur above the confluence of North Grape Creek. A half-mile past the dam, the flow channels to river left and creates nice surfing opportunities up top; but at the bottom left of the rapid lurks a big pourover that has hammered more than one boater. Below North Grape Creek the river swings to the right to form a rapid near some interesting caves and arch formations. A mile downstream just past a camp of three small houses on river right is a rapid whose waves can get up to eight feet high.

The seventeen miles from Johnson City to Pedernales Falls State Park are relatively uneventful for the first half of the run. But starting about nine miles into the run, fun surfing holes appear with increasing frequency. At 3,000 cfs you can play almost nonstop mile after mile. At low water, ledges up to seven feet high create tight slots, and at high water they form grabby hydraulics. The run ends at Pedernales Falls, a sequence made up of a ten-foot ledge, a fifteen-foot slide, and a tight S-turn chute.

In the 1980s whitewater boaters ran the first drop at the falls and took out above the slide (which, at high water, creates a terminal hydraulic). But because

Randy Barnes runs a broken ledge on the Pedernales River

Judd Cherry demonstrates a shudder rudder on the Pedernales River. Photo by Joe Ruszkowski, courtesy Judd Cherry

several tourists drowned when the river was up, park rangers closed the falls to both tourists and boaters at moderate to high water. Now the only way to run this stretch is at low water levels, when visitors at the park are allowed to walk down to the falls. However, even then, swimming is not allowed, so you risk getting arrested if you are caught in the river. In recent years paddlers who

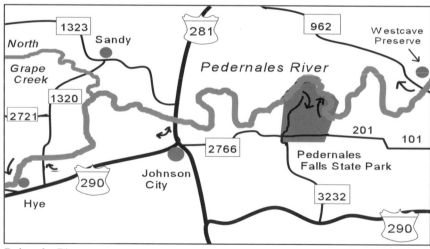

Pedernales River

boof the first drop and bounce down the slide carry their boats up to the parking lot quickly and discreetly.

Below the park is a picturesque fourteen-mile class I–II float trip lined with semitropical plants such as elephant ears. A class II rapid is 100 yards upstream from the takeout at Hammett's Crossing. To get there from the park, take Blanco CR 201/Hays CR 101 to FM 12 and go north to where FM 12 meets FM 3238. There the roads merge into Hamilton Pool Road in Travis County (which becomes FM 962 in Blanco County). Hammett's Crossing is where that road crosses the river just downhill from the Westcave Nature Preserve on the west side of the river and Hamilton Pool on the east.

Running one of North Grape Creek's many ledges. Photo by Bruce Tate

North Grape Creek

Run: FM 1631 to Sandy (FM 1320)		
Location: West of Johnson City	*Counties*: Gillespie, Blanco	*Drainage*: 108 mi² *Length*: 15½ miles
Gradient: 26 ft/mi *Class*: II–III+	*Gauge*: Pedernales River at Fredericksburg, 1,500 cfs (8.7'); at Johnson City, 20,000 cfs (15.2')	

No stream in the state shows up on topo maps as having more rapids per mile than North Grape Creek. More than twenty rapids are marked on the 7½-minute maps, and the constant gradient creates numerous play holes and surfing opportunities. Like the Pedernales into which it flows, North Grape sports several class III drops where ledges up to five feet high create occasional grabby pourovers. In fact, it can best be described as a steeper, more continuous, more scenic, and more intimate version of the Pedernales.

The problem with North Grape is access. Upstream crossings of North Grape and its largest tributary, Willow Creek, occur where statutory navigability is questionable, so the only hassle-free way to run North Grape is to put on below the North Grape–Willow confluence. That means getting permission from a landowner to access the creek.

For the 12.7 miles from the North Grape–Willow confluence to FM 1320, the creek cuts through granite, sandstone, and limestone formations. For seven of those miles it drops a surprising 35 ft/mi. Bluebonnets carpet the hills and bluffs along the stream in the spring, and occasional waterfalls from side creeks add to its enchantment.

During seasons of heavy rain and high water, the barbed-wire fences will be washed away. High flows might make getting to a put-in or FM 1320 impossible, so this is one of those runs best made as the creek is dropping (which

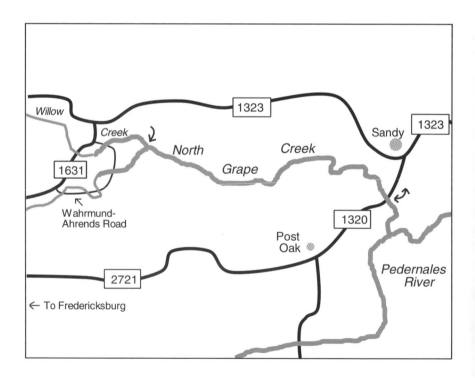

happens very quickly). The two miles from FM 1320 to the Pedernales have some play spots and rapids but lack the gradient and charm of the upper part. Once the creek meets the Pedernales, any sense of intimacy is quickly replaced by the latter's big-water rapids. The takeout is Johnson City.

Cow Creek

Run: FM 1174 to FM 1431		
Location: North-west of Austin	Counties: Burnet, Travis	Drainage: 26 mi² Length: 9½ miles
Gradient: 31 ft/mi Class: III–IV	Gauge: None; use South Fork of San Gabriel, 400 cfs (4.7'); Bull Creek, 200 cfs (4') minimum	

Although close to Austin, this little creek has attracted scant attention. Located in one of the prettiest canyons in Central Texas, Cow Creek combines a solid rock creekbed with a good gradient, numerous drops up to five feet high, and beautiful scenery. Except during extended dry periods, it always has some flow; but like Bull Creek, it can be run only after drenching rains.

Cow Creek Road (Burnet CR 328) runs parallel to the creek and crosses it six times. From most crossings you can get a sense of the creek's potential

Final drop in Cow Creek's picturesque canyon

because just downstream from each is a rapid or interesting drop. The creek occasionally narrows, but even in the first two miles (where the gradient is 40 ft/mi) it is often more than forty feet across.

The creek's constant flow demands that you stay alert, particularly where it threads through willow thickets. Most of the ledges, such as the five-foot drop 200 yards downstream from the second crossing, have chutes or can be punched. Rock jumbles punctuate the run.

As elsewhere, a few barbed-wire fences cross the creek, but they are often washed away after heavy rains. Willow thickets (especially downstream from the second and sixth crossings) occur in the middle of rapids and drops, so the potential for pins and broaches is high. Swimming in any of these very tight and technical spots would be dangerous.

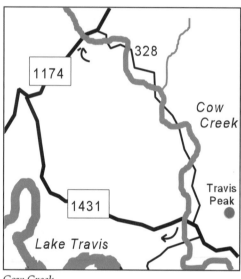

Cow Creek

Most of the low-water crossings are impassable when the creek is running high. Cow Creek Road can be used as the shuttle route only when the creek is at its minimum runnable level and only with high-clearance vehicles. If the road is passable, you will be struck by the area's beauty and might see deer, boar, wild turkeys, roadrunners, and other wildlife. Although action on the creek occupies most of your attention while you are on the water, it is difficult not to be distracted by the scenery.

Because there is no gauge on the creek and none nearby, watch where the rain falls. Periodic rainfall information at Lago Vista and real-time rainfall data at Burnet and Marble Falls are available from Austin's KXAN's Web site (www.aws.com/kxan). Flows on the South Fork of the San Gabriel and Bull Creek also provide rough indicators of rainfall near Cow Creek. If the bottoms of both bridge pillars at the FM 1431 bridge are covered, the creek is runnable. If the water level is high enough to touch the concrete on river left under the bridge, that is even better.

Bull Creek

Run: Spicewood Springs Road to Bull Creek Road (FM 2222)		
Location: Austin	County: Travis	Drainage: 22 mi² Length: 3½ miles
Gradient: 30 ft/mi Class: II–III	Gauge: Bull Creek at Loop 360; 200 cfs (4') low, 1,000 cfs (5.4') high	

Despite its small drainage, Bull Creek is runnable more frequently than its larger Austin counterpart, Barton Creek. Heavy rains in the area can bring it up quickly, but water levels also drop fast (from 2,500 cfs to 250 cfs in four hours). Though the creek drops an average of 40 ft/mi in the three miles above Loop 360 along Spicewood Springs Road, it has few significant drops until below the last road crossing before Loop 360. Most of the gradient drop on the upper stretch occurs at the road crossings themselves (where barbed-wire fences are usually taken out by high water). Unless you like scraping over the edge of asphalt into culvert outflows, probably your best run is from the first Spicewood Springs Road crossing (going up from 360) to FM 2222 (just downstream from Bull Creek Park).

Judd Cherry at Bull Creek's Big One. Photo by Joe Ruszkowski, courtesy Judd Cherry

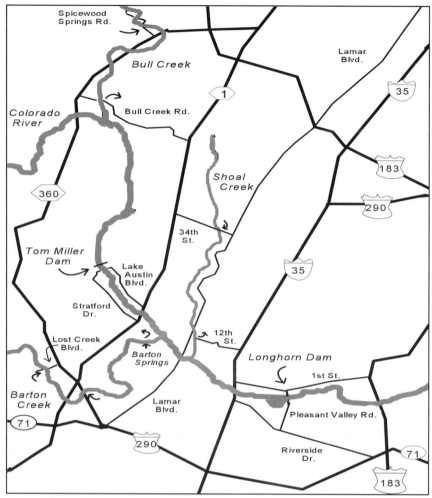

Austin whitewater runs and play spots: Bull Creek, Barton Creek, Shoal Creek, Tom Miller Dam, and Longhorn Dam

The creek has several nice-sized ledges with strong hydraulics at high water. The most noteworthy drop, affectionately called Borés (the "Big One Relatively Speaking"), is just downstream from where the creek passes to the east of the Loop 360 bridge for the second time. A large parking area there attracts crowds when the creek is up. The sneak route is on river left.

Water pouring over from both sides of the V-slot hits the streambed and crashes in the middle to form a standing plume (sometimes five feet high) that you hit head-on if you run the V. The undercut on river right below the V-slot looks nastier than it is. Unless a tree is wedged in it, bodies and boats generally wash through. Needless to say, it is a place to have a good brace and roll.

At high water yahoos often tempt fate by swimming the V-slot without life vests or helmets, proving that natural selection is still at work. If it is a slow news day, they sometimes even attract the attention of local television film crews.

Downstream from Loop 360 the creek can be dangerous because of grabby ledges, strong hydraulics, and groves of small trees in the streambed. Some of the best side surfing, though, is in the last half-mile, so resist the temptation to take out at Bull Creek Park.

Colorado River in Austin (Tom Miller Dam)

Run: Play spot below Tom Miller Dam		
Location: West Austin	County: Travis	Drainage: 27,443 mi² Length: 50 yards
Gradient: Drops four feet Class: II	Gauge: Dam release, 1,700 cfs minimum	

When things really get low, Austin boaters often head to Tom Miller Dam off Lake Austin Boulevard and Stratford Drive on Red Bud Trail. At 1,700 cfs, you can practice ferrying and a little surfing; at 2,400 cfs paddlers in small boats can get enders and squirts and link retentive moves; 3,400 cfs is the maximum generation level.

Release schedules are posted at the LCRA Web site under the Daily River Report (http://www.lcra.org/water/riverrep.html). You can also get the report by calling the LCRA river information line at (800) 776-LCRA. The posted release amount is averaged over twenty-four hours, so if the report says that the release is 1,700 cfs and is scheduled for twelve hours, that means that 3,400 cfs will be released for twelve hours. Though LCRA posts the previous day's release, it does not post the current day's schedule; however,

Backender at Tom Miller Dam © David Abel

releases most often occur in the late afternoon. During droughts, water is released around the clock for downstream irrigation.

Barton Creek

Run: Lost Creek Boulevard to Barton Springs (Zilker Park)		
Location: Austin	County: Travis	Drainage: 103 mi² Length: 7 miles
Gradient: 21 ft/mi Class: II–III	Gauge: Barton Creek at Loop 360; 155 cfs (4') minimum	

Apart from the Guadalupe River below Canyon Dam (which is often crowded with tubers in warmer months), Barton Creek is the most popular run in the state for whitewater paddlers. In a wet year, it is often runnable and stays up for days. Its proximity to Austin and ease of shuttle make it a destination for boaters from as far away as Dallas (when the streams in Arkansas aren't running).

The headwaters of Barton Creek are in Hays County west of Dripping Springs. Along its thirty-five-mile trek to the Colorado River, it meanders into Travis County and ultimately joins the Colorado River in Austin's Zilker Park.

Although whitewater paddlers generally prefer the seven miles from Lost Creek to Barton Springs in Zilker Park, there is also a scenic twelve-mile stretch between SH 71 and Lost Creek Boulevard that is runnable even when the USGS gauge at SH 71 measures as low as 150 cfs. Slightly more difficult than the San Marcos River, the upper part of Barton Creek includes five dams, small rapids (class I–II), and

Todd Swearingen drops into Barton Creek's Twin Falls. © David Abel

C-1er Teresa McFadden enders as Todd Walker waits in the foam at Barton Creek's Twin Falls. Courtesy Carolyn Allbritton

long stretches of flat water. Four miles can be cut off by taking out at Crystal Creek Drive, south of Bee Caves Road.

Near Lost Creek Boulevard the creek's gradient begins to increase. Some of Barton's flow goes underground into the Edwards Aquifer recharge zone, so at 200 cfs on the Loop 360 gauge, the run is scrapy. The first four miles down to Loop 360 contain several small drops, surfing spots, and numerous trees in the channel. A seven-foot dam, one mile downstream from the put-in, can be run cleanly as long as you have sufficient speed to punch the hydraulic at its base. Another mile downstream is Twin Falls, a favorite hang-out for sun worshipers who hike down to the creek from Loop 360 near Barton Creek Mall.

The creek is divided by an island at Twin Falls. The river-right route can be run only at high water. At low to moderate levels, the route on river left culminates in a three-foot drop that forms a tenacious ender spot. Boaters are reluctant to toy with the ender spot these days, because the hole created by the ledge is very aerated and provides little support for bracing if you turn sideways against the ledge. Demonstrating their own version of a mystery move, however, nonboaters sometimes jump into the flow above the drop and pop up twenty feet downstream.

Most Austin paddlers focus on the last three miles of Barton Creek, beginning at Loop 360. Less than one-half a mile downstream is Triple Falls, a

Chris Romine slides into the hole at the second drop of Triple Falls on Barton Creek. Photo by Sheri Romine, courtesy Chris Romine

three-tiered rapid that starts with a technical and sometimes pushy boulder garden, then slides into a pair of fast surfing waves, and ends with a forgiving side-surfing hole. At 3,500 cfs the top hole is very grabby and should generally be avoided. After spending several hours playing at Triple Falls, some boaters elect to carry their boats back up above the first drop and paddle upstream to the parking lot at Loop 360.

In the mile or so downstream from Triple Falls are three of Austin's popular rock-climbing spots: the Urban Assault Wall (river right), and the Gus Fruh and New Walls (river left). The stretch also includes Swirl and Pinball, two challenging rapids ideal for eddy hopping. Below Pinball is the Forest, where willows and sycamores cause havoc to anyone unable to thread through trees in fast-moving water. Then comes Campbell's Hole, at lower flows a rocky technical rapid, at higher flows Grand Canyon–sized waves. Start left and work right to run Campbell's Hole, but don't overlook the opportunities for epic surfs and flamboyant demonstrations of rodeo abilities. The final rapid, Last One, signals that the Barton Springs takeout is just downstream.

An informative guide for Barton Creek is available from the *Austin Chronicle* and at www.auschron.com.

Lagniappe: Although Barton Creek is within the Austin city limits, you hardly know that you are surrounded by urban life. The greenbelt and high limestone bluffs create a sense of isolation that is only occasionally dispelled by the appearance of sunbathers, hikers, and homes high on the bluffs above. After running the quick shuttle right by Barton Creek Mall, you may wonder how you escaped so far so quickly. Expect to see Grumman or Coleman types sacrificing their boats to the creek when it is high.

Shoal Creek

Run: West 34th Street to West 12th Street		
Location: Austin	County: Travis	Drainage: 13 mi² Length: 2 miles
Gradient: 30 ft/mi Class: II–III	Gauge: Shoal Creek at 12th Street, 200 cfs (4.2') low, 1,000 cfs (7.8') high	

Considering the area drained by this creek and the fact that its water is mainly street runoff, it is surprising that Shoal Creek hasn't been completely channeled into a series of big culverts. After a heavy rain, its limestone ledges and rock outcroppings provide some surfing, especially around 24th Street. An occasional cliff and well-manicured backyards add a touch of nature to this downtown run, which passes through the Shoal Creek Greenbelt and Pease Park.

Judd Cherry dives in on Shoal Creek. Photo by Jenny Siebenwer, courtesy Judd Cherry

If you venture farther upstream, watch out for an eighteen-foot waterfall with a nasty hydraulic downstream from Hancock Drive. A low-head dam just north of 24th Street can be a problem at high water. Downstream from 15th Street, just past Pease Park, the creek continues to have some play spots and a fifteen-foot slide near 10th Street. Below the slide is a nasty undercut caused by a washed-away sidewalk. At the 3rd Street railroad bridge a series of pipes has been embedded in the creek two feet apart to catch automobiles before they are swept into the Colorado River. Immediately beyond them is a grabby four-four ledge. Because logs tend to get trapped there, avoid the place.

One final point: wash well when you get home to cleanse yourself of whatever effluent makes it from the streets of Austin into Shoal Creek.

Colorado River in Austin (Longhorn Dam)

Run: Play spot below Longhorn Dam		
Location: Austin	County: Travis	Drainage: 27,600 mi² Length: 50 yards
Gradient: Drops four feet Class: II		Gauge: Tom Miller Dam release, 1,600 cfs minimum

When the releases along the Colorado River are limited to maintaining irrigation downstream, there is usually not enough water coming out of Tom Miller Dam to make surfing interesting. But when there is enough water to surf at Tom Miller, you'll see play possibilities below Longhorn Dam at the east end of Town Lake. It takes the water from Tom Miller a little more than an hour to reach Longhorn (where it simply continues downstream).

A ledge about fifty yards downstream from the dam creates a combination wave hole that is fast and fun, although sometimes hard to stay on. The hole right of center can be a bit grabby because it is formed by a cement wall. It is shallow, and flips there can be especially hard on shoulders. If a number of boaters show up, you may have to wait a few minutes for a shot at surfing the wave—unless you like to see how many boats can fit on it simultaneously.

The setting at Tom Miller is cleaner and prettier than at Longhorn, and some boaters prefer side surfing at Tom Miller at 3,400 cfs. However, the surfing wave at Longhorn is easier to reach, especially when the left-center gate of the dam is open. Austin boaters alternate between the two dam sites.

If you go to Longhorn, park at the softball fields off Pleasant Valley Road on the south side of the river. Since summer releases from Tom Miller Dam are often limited to late afternoon (around 5 P.M.), there is not much time for playing before sundown. During the spring and summer irrigation season, releases happen almost every day.

Lagniappe: A flock of Central American parrots that were released or escaped now nest in the light fixtures above the softball fields at Longhorn. They add a touch of the exotic to an otherwise distinctly urban setting.

Colorado paddler Brian Brown plays at Longhorn Dam. Photo by Breaux Daniel

Onion Creek

Run: William Cannon Drive East to Richard Moya Park		
Location: South Austin	*County*: Travis	*Drainage*: 285 mi² *Length*: 5 miles
Gradient: 12 ft/mi *Class*: II+ (IV)	*Gauge*: Onion Creek at Driftwood, 250 cfs (3.5'); at US 183, 325 cfs (7') minimum	

For years Austin boaters have been interested in the stretch of Onion Creek that cuts through the Balcones Escarpment between Dripping Springs and Buda. The creekbed appears to meet the requirements for statutory navigability (especially west of Buda, downstream from the last FM 150 crossing), but paddlers have faced arrest, attack dogs, and other threats.

A more accessible run is east of I-35, where the creek passes through Mc-Kinney Falls State Park. Upstream from McKinney, a path in Springfield Park runs alongside a small boulder garden rapid. In the state park, the two most notable whitewater features are the creek's two waterfalls. The Upper Falls is eight feet high and can be portaged on the left. Not far downstream, near the confluence of Williamson Creek, ten-foot-high McKinney Falls (a.k.a. Lower Falls) can be portaged on the right. Park officials are not enthusiastic about people running the falls because of the grabby hydraulics. When boaters run either falls, they do so carefully and discreetly.

Below the park there is one more interesting rapid near McKinney Falls Parkway. The take-out is one mile east of US 183 at Richard Moya Park off Burleson Road.

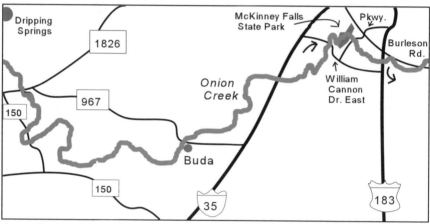

Onion Creek

PART FIVE

~

Guadalupe, San Antonio, and Nueces River Drainages

Randy Barnes enders at Hueco Springs Rapid on the lower Guadalupe River. Courtesy Lauri Barnes

Guadalupe, San Antonio, and Nueces River Drainages

SOME OF THE BEST WHITEWATER STREAMS in Texas originate in the rugged Hill Country northwest of San Antonio. As they fall off the Edwards Plateau, they cut through the Balcones Escarpment, creating scenic canyons and great places to hone boating skills. Their proximity to San Antonio and Austin might suggest that they get paddled frequently. But with the exception of the Guadalupe River and the San Marcos River, most of these runs are known in name only to Texas whitewater boaters.

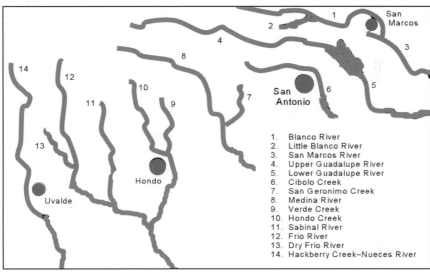

1. Blanco River
2. Little Blanco River
3. San Marcos River
4. Upper Guadalupe River
5. Lower Guadalupe River
6. Cibolo Creek
7. San Geronimo Creek
8. Medina River
9. Verde Creek
10. Hondo Creek
11. Sabinal River
12. Frio River
13. Dry Frio River
14. Hackberry Creek–Nueces River

Guadalupe, San Antonio, and Nueces River whitewater tributaries

Blanco River

Nestled between the drainages of the Pedernales River to the north and the Guadalupe River to the south, the Blanco River is a combination of play spots, drops, and flat water characteristic of its better-known counterparts. Limestone bluffs and overhanging bald cypress corridors make the Blanco a whitewater delight for those lucky enough to catch it up. The scenery is outstanding along its eighty-seven-mile course, especially where it drops through the Narrows, which at high water is one of two true class VI rapids described in this book.

Running the third drop of the Narrows on the Blanco River. Photo by Jimmy Vick

Run: Blanco CR 407 to Fischer Store Road (Hays CR 181)		
Location: Northwest of San Marcos	*Counties*: Blanco, Hays	*Drainage*: 123 mi² *Length*: 16 miles
Gradient: 18 ft/mi *Class*: II–III (one V–VI)	*Gauge*: Blanco at Wimberley, 600 cfs (5.1') minimum	

Numerous surfing spots and rapids occur in the uppermost section from east of the town of Blanco to the Fischer Store Crossing. The whole sixteen-mile run contains enough class II and III rapids to allow eddy hoppers to get a good workout. There is even at least one good ender spot.

The best reason to run this section is to see the Narrows. For whitewater junkies, there is no sight more awesome. When the river is higher than 800 cfs on the Wimberley gauge, the series of drops that comprises the Narrows takes on the character of Poudre Falls or Gorilla on the Green Narrows (but with a terminal hole at the bottom). It can be run only between 450 and 750 cfs (roughly zero to five inches over the put-in bridge), but at those levels other sections of the river are scrapey. Generally, a moderate level for the run (excluding the Narrows) is 1,250 cfs (one foot over the CR 407 put-in bridge).

When the rest of the river is up, the Narrows is terminal. After a runnable five-foot drop into a squirrelly chute that flushes into a large recovery pool, the

Randy Barnes looks for the line in the first drop of the Narrows

river narrows to twenty feet across, drops over an eight-foot ledge into a boiling caldron hemmed in by fifteen-foot vertical walls, and races another ten yards before squeezing through a five-foot-wide double-envelope drop that crashes another ten feet into a violent, exploding nightmare—which, to top it off, is followed just a few yards later by a twelve-foot plunge into a horrifyingly grabby hole. As the river plummets over each drop and cuts farther into the sheer walls, it falls away from any possible rescuer into a netherworld. The slightest misstep above can cast the unwary into its shadows, darkness, and deafening roar.

The river-right portage around this beast brings you right up to a landowner's house (and has been a point of friction in the past). The river-left portage is at least 200 yards over rough terrain and culminates in a chance for you to show off your rock-climbing skills as you head back down to the water.

The Little Blanco River joins the Blanco two miles downstream from the Narrows. The five miles from there to the takeout has an average gradient of 20 ft/mi and contain a half-dozen fun class II and III rapids. Although you might want to stay longer at the Narrows, you should allot enough time to take advantage of these drops and play spots.

Lagniappe: Like Comfort, Boerne, and Wimberley, the historic downtown square of the city of Blanco is filled with quaint crafts and antique shops. To see some three-foot-long dinosaur tracks in the Blanco riverbed, go 3½ miles west of town on FM 1623 and turn south on CR 103. The sauropod footprints are about fifty feet downstream from the crossing. Of course, they are most visible when the river is too low to run.

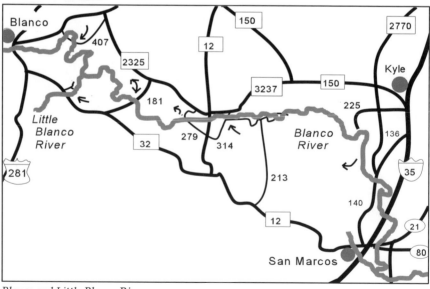

Blanco and Little Blanco Rivers

Run: Fischer Store Road (Hays CR 181) to Wimberley		
Location: Northwest of San Marcos	*County*: Hays	*Drainage*: 238 mi² *Length*: 10 miles
Gradient: 10 ft/mi *Class*: II–	*Gauge*: Blanco at Wimberley, 800 cfs (5.4') minimum	

The ten-mile stretch of the Blanco upstream from Wimberley offers many surfing opportunities—thanks to its solid limestone riverbed. However, it is more memorable for its views of the rugged terrain of Devil's Backbone, a ridge in the Balcones Fault Zone, than its rapids or drops. Crossings above Wimberley can cut off the last three uninteresting miles of this stretch.

Above Lil' Ark on the Blanco River. Photo by Jean McArthur

The twenty-mile stretch from Wimberley to the Five-Mile Dam southwest of the I-35 rest area near Kyle has a number of rapids reminiscent of the forks of the San Gabriel and the Pedernales Rivers. A road on the north side of the river crosses it several times east of Wimberley down to the Lil' Arkansas Camp (which can cut up to seven miles off of this run). This last stretch of Blanco whitewater ends a few miles above where the river joins the San Marcos River east of the city of San Marcos. There is little whitewater from Five-Mile Dam to the rivers' confluence.

Run: Wimberley to Kyle (FM 150)		
Location: Northwest of San Marcos	County: Hays	Drainage: 355 mi² Length: 20 miles
Gradient: 10½ ft/mi Class: II–III		Gauge: Blanco at Wimberley, 800 cfs (5.4') minimum

When the Blanco River crossings near Wimberley are impassable (1,300+ cfs), put in on the low-water crossing just downstream from the Wimberley bridge. In such high-water conditions there are dangerous hydraulics behind two of the crossings downstream (with possible sneak routes on far river right). Between the second nasty crossing and Lil' Ark is a powerful class IV drop with a big hole that can be run on the left by punching diagonal breaking waves. At high water there are wonderful surfing waves and holes throughout the remainder of the run. However, be prepared to thread through groves of trees. Scenery is spectacular, especially after rainstorms, when numerous waterfalls pour off the bluffs along the river.

Little Blanco River

Run: FM 32 to Fischer Store Road (Hays CR 181)		
Location: North of San Antonio	Counties: Blanco, Comal, Hays	Drainage: 69 mi² Length: 6 miles
Gradient: 17 ft/mi Class: II–III		Gauge: Blanco at Wimberley, 3,000 cfs (7.6') minimum

The Little Blanco River is one of the prettiest runs in the state. Shaded by a canopy of cypress trees, its first two miles have a 12 ft/mi gradient and contain a few riffles and small boulder gardens. To get to the whitewater stretch, take Narrows Road on the north side of the river and put in at the Monterrey Drive crossing. From that point downstream, the gradient increases up to 40 ft/mi and rapids are relatively continuous. Several drops involve threading between trees in the middle of rock piles, and two are created by runnable dams. At high flows the surfing holes are deceptively grabby and powerful— just the stuff for aspiring rodeo types. Expect fences except after floods.

A half-mile before the river joins the Blanco, it levels out and passes by high cliffs and caves. Springs and runoff creeks create numerous waterfalls that cascade into the river from fifty feet above.

There is no road access to the confluence. Once you have discovered the joys of the Little Blanco, you have still have the rapids on five miles of the upper Blanco ahead of you. Those five miles drop an average of 20 ft/mi, so you move quickly in what turns out to be an eleven-mile trip.

San Marcos River

Run: Westerfield Crossing to FM 1979		
Location: San Marcos	Counties: Caldwell, Hays, Guadalupe	Drainage: 93 mi² Length: 11½ miles
Gradient: 6 ft/mi Class: I–II	Gauge: San Marcos River at San Marcos, 200 cfs (5.5') minimum	

Many paddlers in Texas get their first taste of whitewater on the San Marcos River because it has year-round flow from Aquarena Springs and because it is home to several outfitters who rent canoes and kayaks. There is not a lot of whitewater among the elephant ears and other subtropical vege-tation. But if you are just learn-ing the intricacies of sweeps, pries, and ferrying, or if you are intimidated by the thought of flipping over in a kayak, the San Marcos's clear, warm (seventy-two degree) moving water fills the bill.

There are small rapids else-where on the river, but white-water boaters are generally attracted either to the six-mile stretch from Westerfield Cross-ing (Caldwell CR 101/Hays CR 266) to FM 1979 or to the Rio Vista Dam in San Marcos (where there is a surfing hole). The run between Westerfield and FM 1979 has some fast

Texas Water Safari racers zip through the San Marcos's Cottonseed Rapid © David Abel

flow with twists and turns but no significant drops (unless you count Martindale Dam, which you portage on the right). Cottonseed Rapid, three miles below Westerfield, is the best spot on the river to see novice boaters spill. Here the river picks up speed, splits around a rock in the center of the rapid, and washes up against a wall on river left. The most interesting way to run it is to enter on the left side and angle to the right at the bottom.

During periods of heavy rain, flows on the San Marcos River rise substantially above its typical 200 cfs due to inflow from the Blanco River. At these higher levels, normally benign low-water crossings and dams create terminal hydraulics, and the clarity of the river is replaced with the brown silt of the Blanco.

Judd Cherry blasts the Rio Vista Dam hole on the San Marcos. Courtesy Chris Romine

Access parking has recently been a problem, especially on the Martindale side of Scull's Crossing. You can avoid being hassled by the Martindale police if you access the river at private campgrounds (e.g., Pecan Park 0.7 miles downstream from Westerfield or Shady Grove Campground at FM 1979). Shady Grove is also where the Spencer Canoes paddling shop is located. If you just have to spend money on boats or gear or just enjoy hanging around paddling shops, check it out. But be careful on SH 80 near Martindale; it is a notorious speed trap.

Lagniappe: In June the San Marcos River is the site of the grueling 265-mile Texas Water Safari.

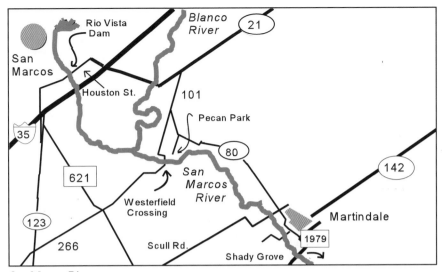

San Marcos River

Upper Guadalupe River

The Guadalupe River is the best-known recreational stream in the state. Most people are more familiar with the popular tubing run below Canyon Lake, the Guadalupe's major impoundment. But above the lake rapids occasionally distract paddlers from the pleasant scenery of the Hill Country.

The Guadalupe is formed by the confluence of its north and south forks in Kerr County near Hunt and empties 464 miles downstream into the Gulf of Mexico at San Antonio Bay. There are really no rapids to speak of on the forks and on the main river above Kerrville; few rapids in the seventy or so miles downriver from Kerrville are more than fast current spots.

Run: Center Point to Comfort (Mill Road off Pankratz Road)		
Location: Northwest of San Antonio	*County*: Kerr	*Drainage*: 839 mi² *Length*: 9½ miles
Gradient: 6 ft/mi *Class*: II (III–)	*Gauge*: Guadalupe at Comfort, 500 cfs (3.5') minimum	

This scenic part of the river is known for its towering cypress canopies, birds, limestone riverbed, and geological formations. Most of the rapids are at the end of long stretches of flat water. The ledges, small dam sites, and rock jumbles that form these class II drops become pushier if the flow is above

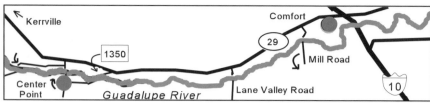

Upper Guadalupe River, Center Point to Comfort

1,200 cfs, but even at high water they hardly merit a class III– rating (although some paddlers will, no doubt, swim them).

A rapid known as Rock Pile (between Government Crossing in Center Point and Lane Valley Road) is the most notable rapid. It consists of an entry with a large number of rocks scattered across the river, with a chute running from the near downstream left bank toward the middle of the river. The rocks create a small dam drop of two feet where standing waves develop above 2,000 cfs. An additional drop of a couple of feet occurs seventy-five yards downstream where the river splits around a large cypress tree.

The seventeen miles from Lane Valley Road to Waring (six miles downstream from Comfort) include several low-water crossings, an old mill race, a small dam, and a ledge that creates a standing wave between 650 cfs and 1,500 cfs. In the fifty-one miles between Waring and FM 3351 are numerous small rapids.

Lagniappe: The bizarre: full-sized stuccoed replicas of Stonehenge and an Easter Island stone head sit out in a field alongside FM 1340 two miles west of Hunt. The sublime: fifteen miles northeast of Comfort, several million bats exit an abandoned railroad tunnel every evening at dusk. Visitors are allowed to get close to the tunnel opening only on Thursday and Saturday.

Run: FM 3351 (formerly FM 3160) to Rebecca Creek Road		
Location: North of San Antonio	*Counties*: Kendall, Comal	*Drainage*: 1,310 mi² *Length*: 23 miles
Gradient: 7 ft/mi *Class*: II	*Gauge*: Guadalupe at Spring Branch, 900 cfs (4.8') minimum	

The most frequently run stretch of the upper Guadalupe begins at Sultenfuss Crossing (FM 3351, formerly FM 3160). Many paddlers set up shuttles and put in at Bergheim Campground. In the first three miles are two named rapids. Rock Pile—not to be confused with the rapid of the same name fifty miles upstream—is a boulder garden often run on the far left near a cypress tree. Dog Leg is a sloping sharp right turn. At moderately high water (e.g.,

3,500 cfs) Rock Pile is all but washed out, but Dog Leg is a riverwide wave. Less than a mile downstream is the Edge Falls crossing, followed by a boulder garden that gets interesting above 2,000 cfs. A few more ledge and boulder drops appear before you reach Guadalupe River State Park at mile 8. Three miles below the park is a sometimes dangerous low-water crossing near Curry Creek.

Most whitewater boaters prefer the last ten miles of the run. Not only does this stretch have the two most challenging drops but it also includes a scenic ten-foot travertine waterfall that cascades into the river. At Mueller Falls (mile 20) most of the river pours over a four-foot ledge on river right, and at Rust Falls (mile 22) the river makes a sweeping left turn over some broken ledges run mainly on river left.

On the upper Guadalupe River above Rebecca Crossing. Photo by Patsy Kott

To cut off the first four miles of this ten-mile run, put in at Guadalupe Canoe Livery at US 281. To do the whole ten miles, park at Specht's Crossing (Old Spring Branch Road, mile 13), where Comal County plans to build a cul-de-sac with parking to the river's edge. If you take out at Rebecca Creek Road, remember that the county right-of-way extends twenty feet upstream and forty-five feet downstream of the bridge. Park on the north side of the river if you can, but watch out for the barbed-wire fence extending into the river. The Guadalupe stalls in Canyon Lake, not far below Rebecca Creek Road.

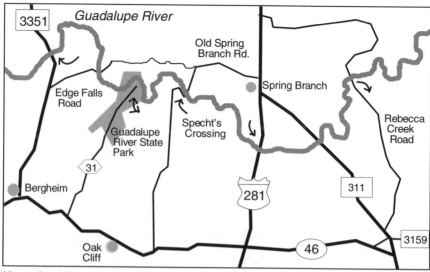

Upper Guadalupe River, FM 3351 to Rebecca Creek Road

Lagniappe: After heavy rains, active caves in the area resonate with the sounds of dripping water. Cave without a Name, eight miles northeast of Boerne, is one of the prettiest and certainly the least commercialized.

Randy Barnes and Steve Daniel surf below the fourth crossing on the Lower Guadalupe at 5,000 cfs. Courtesy Steve Mills

Lower Guadalupe River

Run: Canyon Dam to Cypress Bend Park (New Braunfels)		
Location: Northwest of New Braunfels	County: Comal	Drainage: 1,410 mi² Length: 22 miles
Gradient: 10 ft/mi Class: II (III–)	Gauge: Guadalupe at Sattler (Canyon Dam), 350 cfs (5.2') minimum	

For whitewater boaters the lower Guadalupe is a mix of the best and the worst. Because it is dam controlled and has some interesting rapids, it can be a godsend on hot summer days when everything else is too low to run. When heavy rains upstream cause the lake to rise quickly, releases of up to 5,000 cfs create fantastic surfing waves and rodeo-quality holes.

Unless releases exceed 1,000 cfs, however, thousands of beer-drinking tubers also descend on the river during the summer, especially on weekends, and destroy any sense of a wilderness experience. If you could ignore the crowds, the constant presence of police giving speeding tickets, and the ubiquitous No Parking signs, the lower Guadalupe would be a place of irresistible beauty and fun.

Detailed descriptions of the river and its rapids are available from the local outfitters, which provide rafts, inflatable kayaks, canoes, and inner tubes for the masses. Because the river attracts real novices every day, most descriptions of the rapids are exaggerated. Of course, that is part of the hype that permits campgrounds to charge high fees to access the river. Consider yourself lucky if you can park your vehicle for only $2.

Except during high releases (5,000 cfs), whitewater paddlers focus on the 3½-mile stretch between Hueco Springs Rapid and Gruene Crossing. Above

Rear endering at Hueco Springs Rapid on the lower Guadalupe

Jennifer Murphy plays at Clutter (a.k.a. Cypress) Rapid on the lower Guadalupe © David Abel

Hueco are sixteen miles of mostly flat water occasionally interrupted by dams or rapids with standing waves that can swamp open canoes.

The most dangerous drop on the river is Horseshoe Falls, 1½ miles below the dam. Unless you know how to boof the downstream points of a crescent falls, you probably want to avoid this six-foot drop; most of its flow recirculates back into the ledge. A number of people have died here.

A little less than a mile downstream is the first of eight dams on the river. Most can be run with caution. When the flow is 5,000 cfs, the fastest and deepest wave on the river, along with a bona fide rodeo hole, forms at Dam 4 (mile 6) below the fourth crossing of River Road. At low to moderate flows, S Turn (mile 6.2), Devils Playground (mile 8.5), Bad Rock (mile 9), the Chute (mile 12.3), and Stairstep Rapids (mile 15) require some moves to stay in the main flow.

Dam 6 (mile 16) under the first crossing of River Road is recognized as the start of the best whitewater stretch on the river. The Guadalupe's most popular rapid, Hueco Springs, is a few hundred yards downstream. There the river tumbles through a rock garden and over a three-foot drop mostly to the left of a large boulder midstream. Above 500 cfs an ender spot forms on the river left side of the boulder, along with a squirrelly eddy line. A few yards downstream a side surfing hole attracts boaters intent on improving their 360s. At 1,500 cfs the hole turns into an ender wave; at 2,500 cfs and higher, another ender hole/wave forms just downstream on river right.

During warm months, both sides of the river teem with onlookers who are entertained by boaters showing off their skills at Hueco. Paddlers often stop for lunch to watch tubers lose their bathing suits as they get trashed in the drop. The spot also attracts scuba divers looking for rings, watches, and other items that fall off hapless folks who don't have a clue about the force of the water.

A few hundred yards downstream from Hueco is Slumber Falls, a two-part drop that first kicks boaters with a standing wave, and then turns sharply and plunges over a small dam. The dam is deceptively grabby and has claimed more than one life. At 1,000 cfs I once saw it flip and recirculate a six-person raft. On busy summer days, local rescue teams camp out there and constantly pull people out of the hydraulic. Run it straight on with speed. At high levels the whole rapid is just a flush.

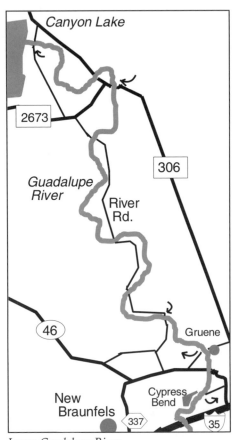

At Clutter (a.k.a. Cypress) Rapid a mile downstream, trees and rocks seem to draw most of the current to river left. The best channel, however, is through a narrow opening on river right at the top of the rapid. Below Clutter is Slant, a great slide to surf if the flow is at least 500 cfs.

Just above the Gruene Crossing low-water bridge is a fast and bouncy rapid named for the crossing. You can practice dynamic eddy hopping or spend hours working on stern squirts on the eddy lines right next to the snack shack by the bridge.

Lower Guadalupe River

In the two miles from Gruene to the takeout at Cypress Bend Park in New Braunfels there is only one named rapid, Dog Leg, where the river winds through large cypress trees. Just before you reach the park you'll encounter a surfing wave below the Common Street bridge; at 1,000 cfs, it is easy to reach and a great place for intermediate paddlers to work on their wave-surfing skills. At 5,000 cfs the wave is smooth, fast, and big enough for several boaters at the same time. If you take out in the small park on river left rather than on river right, you will have more privacy for changing clothes and loading boats.

If you have trouble getting flow data from the USGS Web site, check the Corps of Engineers Web site (http://swf66.swf-wc.usace.army.mil).

Cibolo Creek

Run: Oak Village North (RM 1863) to Luxello (FM 2252)		
Location: Northeast of San Antonio	*Counties*: Comal, Bexar	*Drainage*: 274 mi² *Length*: 18 miles
Gradient: 14 ft/mi *Class*: II	*Gauge*: Cibolo Creek at Selma, 200 cfs; at Boerne, 70 cfs (1.7') minimum	

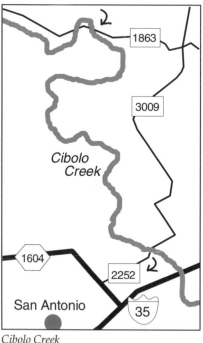

Cibolo Creek

Beginning west of Boerne in Kendall County, Cibolo Creek flows ninety-six miles to its confluence with the San Antonio River in Falls City. After it passes through Camp Bullis and is joined by Balcones Creek, it cuts through a scenic canyon near Natural Bridge Caverns. Rapids are boulder gardens choked by small willows and sycamores.

Just downstream from the put-in is a skeet-shooting range. Unless you want to be a clay pigeon, ask the skeet shooters firing over the creek on river right to hold off while you paddle by. Getting their attention is tough, though, because they inevitably wear hearing protection gear. A shooter once spotted us only after pieces of clay were already raining down around us.

San Geronimo Creek

Run: San Geronimo (Park Road 37) to Cliff (SH 211)		
Location: West of San Antonio	*Counties*: Bexar, Medina	*Drainage*: 86 mi² *Length*: 10½ miles
Gradient: 25 ft/mi *Class*: Probably II–III	*Gauge*: None; use Cibolo Creek at Boerne, 150 cfs (2') minimum; also check Helotes Creek	

Potentially one of best whitewater streams in the state, San Geronimo Creek is nestled in a spectacular canyon less than thirty minutes from San Antonio. Its small drainage has not prevented it from receiving enough water to carve out a sizable solid rock creekbed. If the twelve-foot waterfall just downstream from the put-in is any indication of what this yet unrun creek offers, paddlers will be flocking to it when rains come to the region.

Because the creek is spring fed, it holds water much longer than streams that depend solely on runoff. A week after heavy rains it still seems to have enough water to run the drops and sections that are visible from road crossings and highways. Like other recent Texas whitewater discoveries, this is a creek that paddlers will be astounded has not been explored.

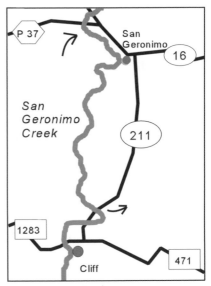

San Geronimo Creek

The flow of the creek increases significantly about a half-mile from the put-in on Park Road 37 where another creek comes in from the hills to the west. After meandering alongside SH 16 (the Bandera Highway) for 1½ miles, the creek turns away from the highway in the hamlet of San Geronimo and begins carving its way down through the Balcones Escarpment. A mile downstream it is backed up by a small dam, and three miles later it passes under a large pipeline. Apart from tidbits gleaned from the topo maps, it is anyone's guess what the run is like. But from what I have seen at the crossings and from the maps, this creek has everything it takes to be a whitewater prize.

Twelve-foot waterfall near the put-in on San Geronimo Creek

Medina River

Run: Three miles east of Medina to FM 470 west of Bandera		
Location: Northwest of San Antonio	County: Bandera	Drainage: 250 mi² Length: 11½ miles
Gradient: 10 ft/mi Class: I–II		Gauge: Medina at Bandera, 250 cfs (5.2') minimum

The most striking things about the 116-mile-long Medina River are its spring-fed crystal clear water and large limestone boulders. Except during dry periods, the Medina usually has enough water to float, but its whitewater is limited to occasional drops created by small limestone ledges and tree roots. At high water, dams, low-water crossings, and occasional rock outcroppings provide some surfing opportunities. But in general the Medina is noteworthy more for its ability to cool you down in the summer than its challenge to your paddling skills. It is a beautiful river for beginners.

Primitive riverside camping is available in the small park on FM 470. It can be used as a takeout, although there are no rapids between it and the day-use only park one-half mile upstream on SH 16. Amenities (for example, rest rooms) are three miles away in Bandera.

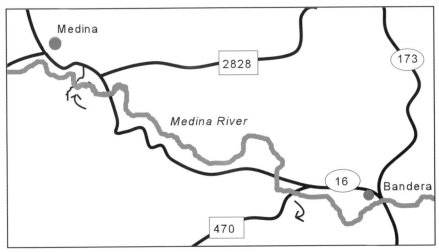

Medina River

The twelve-mile stretch of the Medina from Bandera to Bandera Falls has more water and is not as technical as the upper stretch. At high water its ledges create good surf spots. On hot days you can relax in two large springs on river right a mile upstream from the take-out at English Crossing.

Lagniappe: For apple cider, apple butter, apple ice cream, apple strudel, and apple pie, go to the Love Creek Orchards Cider Mill and Country Store in Medina, the site of the Texas International Apple Festival held in late July.

Roger Smith slips over a drop at low water on the Medina River

Verde Creek

Run: SH 173, third crossing to second crossing north of Hondo		
Location: West of San Antonio	*County*: Medina	*Drainage*: 60 mi² *Length*: 7 miles
Gradient: 28 ft/mi *Class*: II–III		*Gauge*: Hondo Creek at Kings Waterhole, 400 cfs (2.6') minimum

Verde Creek, nestled between the Medina River and Hondo Creek, is a hidden gem only forty minutes from downtown San Antonio. It combines beauty, isolation, and numerous rapids to create one of the most pleasant (though seldomly runnable) intermediate whitewater creeks in the state. Some of the drops (especially "Ziggy," one mile from the put-in) have enough technical features to intrigue advanced boaters and enough overall gradient to raise just about any paddler's heartbeat. Several sycamore groves require that you draw on your slalom skills (which could be quite a challenge in high water), but most of the run is clean and fun. A massive sixteen-foot dam forms a half-mile-long lake a mile from the takeout; portage on the right.

The seven miles below this run (to the first SH 173 crossing north of Hondo) are mostly flat and have many more places where trees clog the main channel.

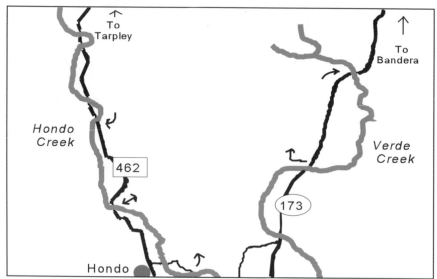

Hondo and Verde Creeks

Hondo Creek

Run: Wade Crossing Waterhole (second FM 462 crossing sixteen miles north of Hondo) to Kings Waterhole		
Location: West of San Antonio	*County*: Medina	*Drainage*: 100 mi² *Length*: 12 miles
Gradient: 6 miles at 15 ft/mi; 6 miles at 19 ft/mi *Class*: Probably II+	*Gauge*: Hondo Creek at Kings Waterhole, 400 cfs (2.6') minimum	

If Verde Creek is running, you probably want to check out Hondo as well. Hondo has a larger drainage than Verde, but it does not have its smaller neighbor's gradient. Above the put-in ten miles south of Tarpley, Hondo drops at a leisurely 14 ft/mi and is impounded by several small dams. As it cuts through the escarpment west of San Antonio, it begins to drop a bit more and should generate some interesting whitewater features. I say "should" because this is another of those runs that no one I know has done. The run can be cut in half where RM 462 crosses the creek ten miles north of Hondo.

When the area has been dry, much of the water from the creek seeps into the Edwards Aquifer before it reaches the Kings Waterhole gauge five miles northeast of Hondo. It is therefore not unusual to see a low flow (e.g., 200 cfs) at Tarpley and absolutely none at Kings Waterhole.

Sabinal River

Run: Utopia (FM 1050) to FM 187 (six miles south of Utopia)		
Location: West of San Antonio	*County*: Uvalde	*Drainage*: 206 mi² *Length*: 8 miles
Gradient: 20 ft/mi *Class*: II	*Gauge*: Sabinal River near Sabinal, 600 cfs (6.3') minimum	

The Sabinal River begins in northwest Bandera County, north of Lost Maples State Natural Area, and flows fifty-eight miles to its confluence with the Frio River in Uvalde County. In the vicinity of Lost Maples, it cuts through Sabinal Canyon (where it drops up to 80 ft/mi). The drainage for this upper section of the river is very small, and much of the rainfall goes into the Edwards Aquifer underground.

FM 187 provides access to the river at several low-water crossings in the four miles between Lost Maples and Vanderpool, but in high water anyone hoping to run the upper stretches will have a long shuttle through Leakey. South of Vanderpool the river drops between 20 and 30 ft/mi for about ten miles before being joined by the West Sabinal River just north of Utopia. The West Sabinal provides additional water for an eight-mile run south of Utopia. That run has a number of ledges and small rapids through cypress stands.

Lagniappe: In the fall (when there is little chance of a run on the Sabinal), the trees of Lost Maples are resplendent with color. As far as amenities in Vanderpool go, don't expect much; the people who put together *The Roads of Texas* forgot to mark this hamlet (population 20) on the map.

Frio River

Run: FM 1050 south of Leakey to SH 127 (Concan)		
Location: West of San Antonio	*County*: Uvalde	*Drainage*: 389 mi² *Length*: 12 miles
Gradient: 16 ft/mi *Class*: II–III		*Gauge*: Frio River at Concan, 500 cfs (4.6') minimum

Known for its spring-fed clarity and limestone bluffs, the Frio River flows for 250 miles through the picturesque Hill Country west of the Sabinal River.

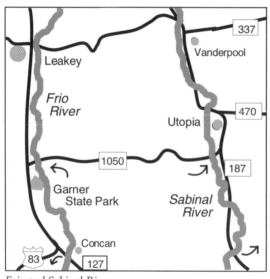

Frio and Sabinal Rivers

Its gradient and drainage make it one of the best play rivers in the state after heavy rains. High water creates numerous waves for surfing, though it also requires that you thread your way through cypress stands. For boaters familiar with it, a high-water run on the Frio is a joy that is all too rare.

Less than two miles below the put-in at FM 1050 is a dam at Garner State Park that can be run with care on the far left. Between there and the

Mary Ann Bauknecht drops over one of the Frio's ledges. Courtesy Tony Plutino

takeout, three low-water crossings and a four-foot waterfall spice up the run with big waves and occasionally grabby holes. Most of the whitewater action occurs downstream from the CR 350 crossing four miles from Concan. At high water another crossing two miles upriver from Concan creates a terminal hydraulic. Unless the high water has recently taken out the fences, expect to encounter some barbed wire.

Wonderful surf spots abound in the quarter mile downriver from Concan. They are well worth the paddle and carry back upstream. The seven miles from Concan to RM 2690 are scenic and often covered by towering cypress trees. Due to its 22 ft/mi gradient, the river moves nicely but it has little whitewater.

Dry Frio River

Run: US 83 to RM 2690		
Location: North of Uvalde	*County*: Uvalde	*Drainage*: 132 mi² *Length*: 12 miles
Gradient: 17 ft/mi *Class*: II–III (IV)	*Gauge*: Dry Frio River at Reagan Wells, 500 cfs; Frio River below Dry Frio, 2,000 cfs minimum	

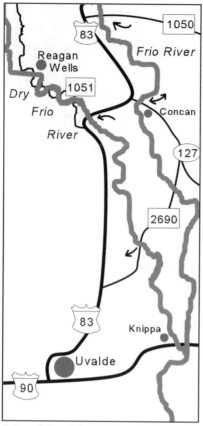
Frio and Dry Frio Rivers

The Dry Frio River is probably one of the top five whitewater play runs in the state. Like Hondo Creek and the Frio River, the Dry Frio typically has some flow on the Edwards Plateau before it cuts down through the escarpment and loses much of its water to the Edwards Aquifer. But after heavy rains the Dry Frio sports numerous surfing waves and holes as it winds through a series of remote picturesque canyons.

From the river you can see traffic on US 83 at two locations. Both signal the approach of class III– rapids. Then things flatten out for a bit as you turn into the hills away from the highway. For a mile or so the river offers only ripples and small waves. Then a string of challenging drops and wave trains spice things up nicely. Two miles from the takeout, the river emerges from the hills, but the play spots keep coming. Just when you think the day is done, you reach Twilight, one-half mile from the takeout.

At 1000 cfs or more, Twilight is the kind of waterfall that is definitely rare in Texas. Dropping ten feet through huge boulders into nasty looking holes, it funnels most of the river toward the hero route in the unscoutable left channel, where the water plunges into a deep hole that precedes an exploding eddy. Most sane paddlers choose the straightforward right channel or slip diagonally from center to left behind the boulders that guard the entrance to the left channel. A grabby ledge 100 yards downstream is Twilight's Last Gleam. Surf waves and play holes continue for another quarter mile.

If you have only a day to max out your fun meter in the Frio River area, don't miss the chance to paddle the Dry Frio. You can combine both by running the Frio from CR 350 to below Concan in the morning and then run the Dry Frio in the afternoon. That way, you arrive at Twilight as the sun is going down. If you can stay two days, gather all your boater friends into an eight-person cabin at Neal's Lodges overlooking the Concan crossing [phone (210) 232-6118]. The office at Neal's even has a computer hookup to the Internet so that you can check water levels of other runs in the area.

C-1er Carolyn Allbritton jumps on one of the Dry Frio's surfing waves

Hackberry Creek–Nueces River

Run: FM 335 Hackberry Crossing to FM 335 Nueces Crossing		
Location: Southwest of Junction	*Counties*: Edwards, Real	*Drainage*: 100 mi² *Length*: 11 miles
Gradient: 8 miles at 23 ft/mi, 3 miles at 15 ft/mi *Class*: Probably II–III	*Gauge*: Nueces near Laguna, 2,000 cfs; also use Frio River at Concan, 1,000 cfs (5') minimum	

Hackberry Creek is one of the two main forks of the Nueces River. Its headwaters are near Rocksprings and Devil's Sinkhole State Natural Area. Before it meets the East Prong of the Nueces River to form the main Nueces at the hamlet of Hackberry, it cuts through a marvelously scenic canyon. Its isolation may explain why this is yet another creek that awaits a first descent.

When the Nueces floods, Hackberry is runnable. Small trees sprout from its rocky drops and ledges, and numerous barbed-wire fences crisscross it. You have to hope that the flood has taken out the fences or that you are good enough to avoid them and the maze of broaching possibilities.

Accessing the creek is a challenge. Don't even try to come in from Uvalde on SH 55; the Nueces covers two of the low-water bridges you have to cross to get to Hackberry. Instead, if you come in from the north on FM 335, you will reach the creek five miles south of SH 41. If the FM 335 crossing prevents you from driving across the creek at the put-in, you'll have to hitch a ride back with a local (or bike shuttle your boat back to the put-in). The takeout is the next FM 335 low-water crossing, five miles north of Vance.

Hackberry Creek–Nueces River

From the confluence of the two forks, you paddle for three miles on the Nueces to reach the takeout. In high water this upper part of the Nueces has some good surfing waves due to its rock and gravel streambed.

Because the Nueces gauge at Cotulla is too far downstream to give you a sense of what is happening up on Hackberry, you should consult the Frio gauge at Concan instead. Because that gauge is forty miles away, paddling is likely only if the whole region gets pounded. You can get a sense of rainfall by consulting the rain gauges twenty-two miles northwest of Rocksprings (NWS TX3 code: SRA) and on the Erikson Ranch near the headwaters of the West Nueces River (TX2 or TX3 code: CAY).

PART SIX

~

Rio Grande Drainage

The Sentinels near Mesa Juan Botas, sixty-four miles downriver from La Linda, Rio Grande Lower Canyons. Courtesy Desert Sports

Rio Grande Drainage

THE RIVERS OF WEST TEXAS MAY NOT HAVE A LOT of whitewater, but they cut through some spectacular canyons (some 1,800 feet deep) and offer boaters a chance to get away for multi-day trips sprinkled with occasionally interesting drops. The best-known of those rivers is, of course, the Rio Grande, especially in and near Big Bend National Park. But two of its major tributaries, the Pecos River and the Devils River, also cut through remote desert canyons and provide river runners great opportunities to get away from it all. These latter rivers attract fewer people, and, unlike the Rio Grande, you do not need permits to run them.

Rio Grande, Boquillas Canyon.
Courtesy Desert Sports

When the rivers and creeks in West Texas get heavy rain (which is not that often), they can become torrents full of play possibilities. To paddle tributaries of the Rio Grande (such as Alamito Creek and Terlingua Creek) you need luck or a willingness to live there. After the rains (especially from November to April), springs in the area often maintain river flows for weeks. Most boaters

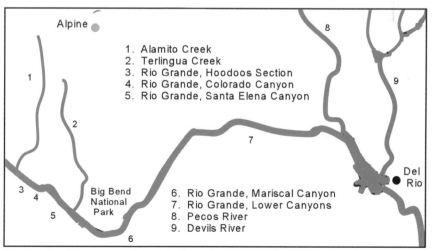

Rio Grande whitewater sections and tributaries

take advantage of the Rio Grande during the fall and spring. Thanksgiving week and the weeks of spring break are the busiest times, and you face limited camping options and must compete for first-come, first-served permits.

Alamito Creek

Run: Casa Piedra to FM 170		
Location: North-east of Presidio	*County*: Presidio	*Drainage*: 1,563 mi² *Length*: 23 miles
Gradient: 37 ft/mi *Class*: Probably III–IV	*Gauge*: Rio Grande five miles southeast of Presidio, minus Rio Grande at Presidio, 500 cfs minimum	

As far as I can determine, Alamito is another unrun creek that will one day attract some adventurous soul. Most of the time it is a wide arroyo with a sand and gravel streambed. But if Marfa and the area south get heavy rains, the creek could be running. It usually takes about twenty-four hours for the water to get from Marfa to Presidio. If you see that the roads south of Marfa are flooding, Alamito will be running for at least a day.

From Plata (at the end of the paved stretch of FM 169 northeast of Presidio) to the next access point at Casa Piedra, the creek drops 34 ft/mi for ten miles. At Casa Piedra the creek heads west and the mountains begin to close in. Ten miles downstream from Casa Piedra, Cienega Creek adds sub-

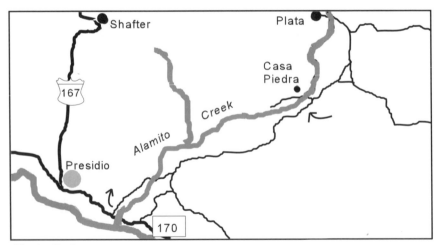

Alamito Creek

stantially to the flow where Alamito cuts through a gorge at 50 ft/mi for three miles and returns to that gradient in the last two miles.

The topos suggest that the combination of water, constriction, and boulder debris from Cienega Creek could make the gorge a place where things could get really interesting. To make this exploratory run will require a real commitment. Not only is it remote and hard to catch, but it would probably require perfect timing. The dirt-road shuttle to the east of the creek is thirty miles each way. And anyone paddling it for the first time would have to hope that it holds its water throughout its twenty-three-mile length. There are dirt road crossings at miles 17½, 19, and 20.

For flow information, call the Presidio office of the International Boundary Waters Commission at (915) 229-3751. During nonbusiness hours, check http://dryline.nws.noaa.gov/afos_data/ RVA/LBBRVALBB.

Terlingua Creek

Run: Agua Fria Road to FM 170		
Location: west of Big Bend National Park	County: Brewster	Drainage: 1,090 mi² Length: 23 miles
Gradient: 27 ft/mi Class: III–IV	Gauge: None; 4' on the FM 170 bridge is a good play level	

This arroyo gets run with some regularity because the Big Bend raft guides who live in Terlingua can jump on it when heavy rains up north cause it to flood. In the sixteen miles from Agua Fria Road to South County Road at Three Bar Ranch, the creek drops over numerous ledges and falls as it passes Agua Fria Peak. A second possible put-in is the low-water crossing three miles downstream from Agua Fria Road.

The seven-mile stretch from Three Bar Ranch to FM 170 east of Terlingua has some nice surfing waves and holes and is the most often paddled part of the creek. However, at South County Road, Three Bar Ranch has tried to close access to the creek. That means paddling the technical upper stretch generally commits a boater to take out elsewhere. Local boaters often get permission to access the creek south of the Three Bar crossing. For more information, contact Far Flung Adventures at (800) 359-4138.

The sixteen miles from the bridge to the Rio Grande takeout of the Santa Elena Canyon run is class II, scenic, and fast-moving due to its 26 ft/mi gradient.

To reach the creek, turn on Agua Fria Road at the Frontier Store on SH

118, twenty-six miles north of the 170 intersection (or fifty-seven miles south of Alpine, just south of the Longhorn Ranch), and go 3½ miles west. To reach Three Bar Ranch, turn off SH 118, eleven miles south of the Frontier Store on North County Road. The takeout at FM 170 is good, but boaters who have received permission to put on the creek from property south of Three Bar often take out a little more than a mile past FM 170 on School Road, which runs parallel to FM 170 from Study Butte to Terlingua. In rainy weather, use a four-wheel drive vehicle on this road.

There is no gauge on Terlingua Creek, but you can estimate its flow by comparing the difference between the Rio Grande gauge at Lajitas and the Rio Grande gauge at Castolon. The level at the Lajitas gauge is generally a little more than one-half foot above the Castolon gauge. The difference diminishes depending on how much water Terlingua pumps in. Of course, the simplest way to find out about flow on the creek is to call one of the Terlingua outfitters.

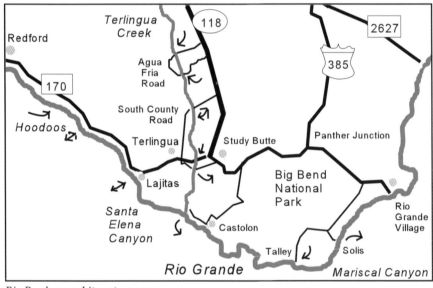

Big Bend area whitewater runs

Rio Grande

Near its headwaters in Colorado, the Rio Grande begins with challenging whitewater, mellows out for 100 miles, and then crashes through canyons in northern New Mexico before either being siphoned off for irrigation or meandering for 1,248 more miles as the border between Texas and Mexico.

When combined with water from the Rio Conchos just upstream from Presidio, it usually has enough flow to create whitewater in the canyons of the Big Bend. But don't expect the same kind of big drops you'd find in New Mexico; even in the canyons the average gradient is only about 5 ft/mi.

Flow information: Although water levels in the different canyons of Big Bend vary substantially in periods of flash flooding, paddlers often refer to the Rio Grande Village gauge (upstream from Boquillas Canyon) to get a sense of what the river is doing. This is what the gauge readings mean:

Gauge height	Cfs flow	Level
2'	300	very low
2.5–3.5'	500–1,000	low
4–6'	1,600–4,100	optimal
7'	5,600	high

A very low run may be all someone on a lightly loaded canoe wants. For someone prepared for whitewater, enough water to get down the river is simply not enough. That is the reason my suggestions about how to interpret the flow rates lean toward more rather than less water.

For the runs above the lower canyons, I recommend checking other Rio Grande gauges upstream at Presidio, Lajitas, Castolon, and Johnson's Ranch, as well as the one downstream near Dryden. Especially if you are curious about the steeper, more technical feeder creeks (e.g., Maravillas, San Francisco, or Sanderson), refer to these other gauges. To find out about all of the gauge readings

- Consult the Web site for Desert Sports in Terlingua (www.desertsportstx. com/DS/BBdaily.html), which is updated daily Monday through Friday. The toll-free phone number is (888) 989-6900.
- Call Big Bend National Park at (915) 477-2252, ext. 188, or (915) 477-2251 and talk to the ranger after the automated recording.
- Call the Midland-Odessa National Weather Service office at (915) 563-5006.
- Call the IBWC office in Presidio at (915) 229-3751. The IBWC Web site (www.ibwc.state.gov/flowdata.htm) is updated twice a week. Because the IBWC reports flow in cubic meters per second, multiply their figure by 35.31 to determine flows in cubic feet per second (cfs).

Some of the Rio Grande gauges—for example, the two at Presidio (one below the Rio Conchos and Cibolo Creek, the other below Alamito Creek five miles southeast of Presidio) and those at Johnson's Ranch near Mariscal Canyon and at Dryden—are automated to provide flow data without being checked manually. The gauges at Lajitas, Castolon, and Rio Grande Village are checked manually, usually every day.

Hoodoos Section

Run: five miles above Colorado Canyon put-in		
Location: Big Bend Ranch State Natural Area	County: Presidio	Drainage: 63,547 mi² Length: 5 miles
Gradient: 6 ft/mi Class: II–III	Gauge: Presidio, 3.5' minimum, 5–8' optimal	

Below the confluence of Alamito Creek near Redford, the Rio Grande begins to show signs that its long drift through southern New Mexico and extreme West Texas is about to be interrupted by the canyons of the Big Bend. The first sign of change appears in the intimate and less frequently paddled Hoodoos stretch. Here the river sports several big, fun rapids and, at higher water, opportunities for playing and surfing abound.

The real attraction of the run are the Hoodoos, spires of eroded igneous rock (sometimes called the Anvil and Davit Rocks) that rise on the north side of the river 2½ miles upstream from the Colorado Canyon River Access in the Big Bend Ranch State Natural Area.

A four-wheel drive road from FM 170 leading to the Hoodoos themselves is blocked off, but you can pull off the highway and walk the 300 or so yards down to see them. You could also carry your boat down, but the whitewater portion of the run is in the three miles upstream.

It is possible to put on the river from the highway by going down a steep embankment three miles east of Redford. At that spot there is a quarter-mile sliver of land owned by the state, but no fence indicates the boundary between private and public land. Or you can paddle an extra seven miles of flat water by putting in at Redford.

However you access the river, remember that in Big Bend Ranch State Natural Area, you must get a river permit either at the Warnock Environmental Education Center in Lajitas [phone (915) 424-3327] or the Fort Leaton State Historic Site near Presidio [phone (915) 229-3613].

Colorado Canyon

Run: Rancherías Canyon to Lajitas		
Location: Big Bend Ranch State Natural Area	County: Presidio	Drainage: 66,000 mi² Length: 21 miles
Gradient: 5 ft/mi Class: II+	Gauge: Rio Grande at Lajitas, 3.5' minimum; 5–7' optimal	

The nice thing about Colorado Canyon is its accessibility. FM 170 (a.k.a. Ranch Road 170) runs next to the river for much of the way, and there are several access points. Rapids are generally rock garden or wall-shot types with occasional surfing possibilities. Intermediate-skilled paddlers often begin their

visit to Big Bend with a warm-up run through the canyon. Colorado is not as closed in as Santa Elena or Mariscal Canyons, but it is scenic in its own way. In contrast to the limestone canyons in Big Bend National Park, Colorado Canyon's walls are of igneous rock from the Sierra Rica and Bofecillos Volcanoes.

The ten-mile stretch between Rancherías and Madera (Monilla) Canyons

National Park Service ranger in Colorado Canyon of the Rio Grande. Courtesy Michael Van Winkle

includes the Rancherías, Closed Canyon, Quarter Mile, Panther, and Madera Canyon Rapids. To run another class II+ drop, Ledgerock Rapids, take out at Grassy Banks (mile 13). In the 8½ miles between Grassy Banks and Lajitas there is only one named rapid (Fresno), a class II–III at certain levels. But to make the stretch more interesting, check out the *Contrabando* movie set three miles downstream from Grassy Banks.

As in the Hoodoos section, you have to obtain a permit to paddle the river either at the Warnock Environmental Education Center in Lajitas [phone (915) 424-3327] or the Fort Leaton State Historic Site near Presidio [phone (915) 229-3613]. At those offices you will receive the standard warnings about not leaving your vehicle unattended, but problems with theft or vandalism are no worse here than most other places.

Santa Elena Canyon

Run: Lajitas to Terlingua Creek		
Location: Big Bend National Park	County: Brewster	Drainage: 69,251 mi² Length: 17 miles
Gradient: 5 ft/mi Class: II (III+)	Gauges: Rio Grande at Lajitas, 3.5' minimum; 5–7' optimal	

After all the hype you hear about Rockslide Rapid, you will definitely want to check out Santa Elena Canyon. Go to experience its towering vertical walls and occasional play spots. Enjoy the chance to eddy-hop down through the canyon's most famous river feature, and be amused by the sight of heavily loaded canoes and rafts being wrapped or portaged.

If you get an early enough start, you can do the run in a day and still explore some of the picturesque side canyons. Since you have to have a national park permit, plan to be at the Lajitas Trading Post when it opens at 8 A.M. to be on the river by 9 A.M. Make sure you have all the standard equipment (flotation, approved life vests, spare paddle, etc.) and that you have made arrangements for the shuttle (fifty miles each way).

Rockslide Rapid in Santa Elena Canyon. Courtesy Desert Sports

It will take at least three hours to paddle the twelve miles of relatively flat water that precedes the canyon. Overnight trips typically camp at the canyon's mouth to avoid having to run Rockslide Rapid in the late afternoon. Other campsites are located farther downstream in the canyon.

Rockslide Rapid is less than a mile inside the canyon. Scout it on the Mexican side; portage on the Texas side (except at high water). Navigating the rapid requires crisp eddy-turns and ferries, so expect to see boats-and-bodies carnage, especially at high water.

Mariscal Canyon

Run: Talley to Solis Landing		
Location: Big Bend National Park	County: Brewster	Drainage: 67,712 mi² Length: 10 miles
Gradient: 5 ft/mi Class: II		Gauge: Rio Grande at Johnson's Ranch, 4' minimum, 5–8' optimal

Like other runs in Big Bend you need to have a permit for Mariscal, but the canyon walls (up to 1,800 feet high) make this spectacular day trip worth the effort. What Mariscal lacks in whitewater it makes up for in scenery and the feeling of isolation. Its walls also contain layers of sedimentary rock that angle up from the river in a way that makes it seem as if you are traveling downhill much faster than you are. Because it is not that far from the major campground in the Park (Rio Grande Village), it is a standard must-do run in the Big Bend.

Randy Barnes slips through Mariscal Canyon's Tight Squeeze. Courtesy Lauri Barnes

Except at high water, two rapids in the canyon are the only places where you need to exercise real boat control. Rock Pile is 1½ miles from the put-in (100 yards inside the canyon); run left of the center boulder. The fifteen-foot-wide Tight Squeeze is one-half mile farther along. Run it on the right side and make a quick left turn to avoid a submerged rock. Two miles downstream the canyon opens up and a creek enters from the Mexican side. Indian petroglyphs can be found on the boulder near the mouth of the creek. Shortly thereafter the canyon constricts, and the feeling of intimacy resumes for four more miles. The takeout is 2½ miles after you leave the canyon.

Lower Canyons

Run: La Linda to Dryden Crossing		
Location: Big Bend National Park	Counties: Brewster, Terrell	Drainage: 70,825 mi² Length: 83½ miles
Gradient: 5 ft/mi Class: II–III (III+)	Gauge: Rio Grande at Rio Grande Village, 2.5' minimum, 4–7' optimal	

The remote and scenic Lower Canyons have been a favorite of river runners for years. For a week you get away from it all without having to spend much money. Beautiful hikes, hot springs, deep canyons, and a chance to spend time with your companions are what make the trip one of the best-known paddling destinations in the state. If you are looking for lots of white-water, go elsewhere. This is a float-the-river-and-enjoy-the-scenery trip that provides few opportunities for practicing your eddy-hopping and ferrying skills through rapids that are all too infrequent for whitewater junkies.

As with other multi-day runs in the West, the Lower Canyons attract rafts and heavily loaded canoes. Ratings for the rapids are often exaggerated—to indicate the difficulty of muscling barges through technical boulder gardens.

Mike Farrell at Hot Springs Rapid, Lower Canyons of the Rio Grande. Photo by Mike Gagner, courtesy Steve Mills

David Reichert and Jennifer Van Winkle bounce through Rodeo Rapid in the Lower Canyons of the Rio Grande. Courtesy Michael Van Winkle

At high flows play spots and surfing waves can provide amusement, but be skeptical when you hear people throw around comments that make the Lower Canyons sound like a Texas version of the Grand Canyon.

You must have a permit and get your equipment (e.g., life vests, floatation, etc.) checked out to paddle this designated Wild and Scenic River. Pick up the permit at the ranger station at Persimmon Gap. During busy seasons like Thanksgiving week and spring break, the limited number of permits may go quickly. If in doubt about your prospects, call the ranger station at (915) 477-2393.

Plan to take day hikes. There are Indian petroglyphs in Bourland Canyon (mile 6) and in caves on the Mexican side of the river back upstream from Maravillas Rapid (mile 11). Another Indian cave is at Middle Watering (Mexico, mile 75). Ruins of Asa Jones's wax factory remain at mile 38 (Silber Canyon), where there are also springs on both sides of the river. Fresh water is available there, in San Rocendo Canyon (mile 41), and just below Lower Madison Rapid (mile 57). Numerous other side canyons also beckon to be explored.

Notable rapids include Hot Springs (mile 41), Rodeo (mile 50), Upper Madison (mile 55), Lower Madison (mile 57), and Agua Verde (mile 82). Only Upper Madison can truly be said to be Class III+ (except, of course, if you have a loaded canoe or raft).

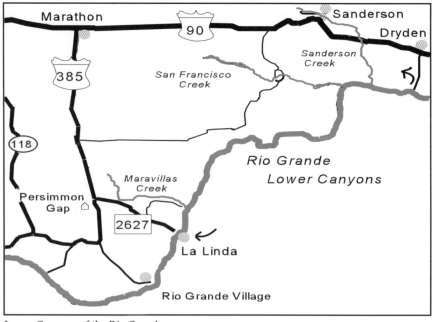

Lower Canyons of the Rio Grande

Heath Canyon near La Linda, Lower Canyons, Rio Grande. Courtesy Desert Sports

Although canoes can get down the run as low as 2 feet on the Rio Grande Village gauge, a minimum whitewater level would be 2½ feet, with 4½ to 7 feet being optimal. Paddlers unfamiliar with serious whitewater could find this "optimal" range intimidating. Above 7 feet, the rapids are either washed out or really interesting.

When the area has been inundated and the river is above 10 feet, start scouting out some of the feeder streams, such as Maravillas Creek (drainage 758 sq. mi.), San Francisco Creek (drainage 628 sq. mi.), and Sanderson Creek (drainage 358 sq. mi.). I know of no one who has run any of them.

Normally the Dryden gauge is about one foot higher than the Rio

Grande Village gauge; when the Rio Grande Village gauge reads 2½ feet, the Dryden gauge is about 3½ feet. If there is a significant difference between the two, either a lot of rain has fallen in the feeder streams or a surge on the river is finally reaching the Dryden takeout.

Because the shuttle distance for this run is so great, it is often best to arrange to have someone move your vehicles for you. It is more than worth the expense. Consider Scott Shuttle Service, (800) 613-5041 or (915) 386-4574, or check their Web site at www.bigbend.com/river. For detailed information on running the river, see *The Lower Canyons of the Rio Grande* by Louis Aulbach and Joe Butler.

Pecos River

Run: Pandale to Pecos River Marina		
Location: North- west of Del Rio	*County*: Val Verde	*Drainage*: 34,601 mi² *Length*: 61 miles
Gradient: 9 ft/mi *Class*: II (III)	*Gauge*: Pecos at Pandale, 225 cfs minimum, 600 cfs optimal	

From its headwaters in New Mexico to its confluence with the Rio Grande near Del Rio, the Pecos River flows more than 500 miles. Much of its course is through semiarid rangeland where rapids are almost nonexistent. In the fifty-eight miles from Iraan to the mouth of Independence Creek, there are a few rapids where side canyons meet the river.

In rainy seasons or after downpours, Independence Creek can contribute a substantial flow to the Pecos. Due to its drainage area (770 sq. mi.) and gradient (20 ft/mi), Independence Creek itself might be worth investigating. Access is not difficult because roads cross it at several places and often run parallel to it. There is no stream flow gauge on the creek, but hourly rainfall data near it can be checked at http://precip.fsl. noaa.gov/hourly_precip.html.

For forty miles below the mouth of Independence Creek, the Pecos flows through increasingly rugged canyonlands. Rapids are still infrequent—mostly boulder gardens where side canyons come in—but the added water makes paddling easier.

The put-in for the most frequently run section is at Bed Rock Ford on Langtry Road southwest of Pandale (off Ranch Road 1024). You can also reach that crossing from the south by driving thirty miles from Langtry on the same gravel road. As with the Lower Canyons of the Rio Grande and the Devils River, it is best to have someone shuttle your vehicles.

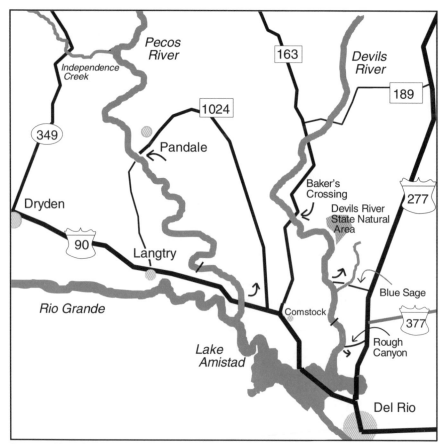

Pecos and Devils Rivers

From Pandale to the Rio Grande, the Pecos cuts through one long canyon that opens up periodically to reveal spectacular vistas. Rapids are clusters of boulders and a few places where ledges channel the river to one side or the other. Between miles 17 and 24 the river broadens out and has carved "flutes," or wagon tracks, in the limestone. At low water the abrasive limestone can really tear up a boat. Try to stay in the narrow channels. If you get out of your boat to drag it, be careful not to step into the cracks.

The most notable rapids are Pin Rock (mile 30; go left of the island), Lewis Canyon (mile 39), Waterfall (mile 39.5), and Painted Canyon (mile 44). Painted Canyon (a.k.a. Hail Mary) Rapid is more technical than any other rapid on the river. It consists of three drops spread out over 100 yards chock-full of boulders. Negotiating it with a fully loaded canoe without pining or swamping is definitely an accomplishment, but the rapid is only class III+.

All along the Pecos are remnants of prehistoric habitation, and all of these sites are on private property. If you want to explore the best places for pictographs and petroglyphs (such as Harkell, Still, Lewis, and Painted Canyons), get permission.

Drinking water is available at Goat Spring (mile 16.7, river right), Everett Spring (mile 18, fifty yards inside Everett Canyon), and an unnamed spring (mile 33, in the rocks near the cane bank, river left).

A weir dam at mile 46, site of the Langtry gauge, indicates the trip is nearly over. Three miles downstream is the spot you should arrange to meet a pickup boat to tow you across twelve miles of Lake Amistad to the takeout. The winds on the lake can be brutal. For shuttle and boat pickup, contact Manuel or Inez Harwick of High Bridge Adventures at (915) 292-4495.

Joe Riddell paddles an inflatable kayak through Painted Canyon Rapid on the Pecos River
© *David Abel*

Current flow information (updated every three hours) is available from the IBWC Del Rio office [phone (830)-775-2437] in cubic meters per second. Multiply that figure by 35.31 to get the equivalent cfs. The gauge height also provides information about the flow—for example, 1.55 ft (0.515 m) equals 152 cfs. To check rainfall upstream at Sheffield (NWS code: SIC), consult the Lubbock NWS Web site at http://dryline.nws. noaa.gov/other_afos_data/ NMC/RRA/TX2, TX3, or MAF.

For detailed information on running the river, see *The Lower Pecos River* by Louis Aulbach and Jack Richardson.

Teresa and David McFadden run Waterfall Rapid on the Pecos. Courtesy Tony Plutino

Devils River

Run: SH 163 to Rough Canyon Marina		
Location: North of Del Rio	*County*: Val Verde	*Drainage*: 2,876 mi² *Length*: 47 miles
Gradient: 10 ft/mi *Class*: II+ (IV)	*Gauge*: Devils River at Pafford, 225 cfs minimum, 500 cfs optimal	

The Devils River is another scenic, West Texas multi-day trip that contains interesting rapids spaced out all too infrequently. Although the river flows for approximately 100 miles, only the last fifty or so stay above ground with any consistency (except when everything is flooding). Several small rapids appear in the stretch downstream from Baker's Crossing, and four larger stair-step drops often swamp open canoes, providing whitewater boaters entertainment amid the natural splendor.

Known for its vistas and Indian pictographs, the Devils River jostles along at a nice 15 ft/mi for twenty miles from the put-in. Its most dramatic plunge occurs sixteen miles into the trip at Dolan Falls, a twelve-foot vertical drop that, at high water, contains nasty hydraulics. Other rapids are plain fun: scrapey at low water, pushy at high.

Much of the river has a wide limestone bottom with wagon-wheel ruts that parallel the flow and promise sprains and breaks to anyone making the slightest misstep. At low water the abrasive limestone grinds away at boats and at the shoe soles of paddlers having to drag their usually overloaded boats across rocky shoals. Open stretches of river are often followed by willow and reed thickets; if you choose the wrong passage here, you have to pull your boat back to channels through leech-infested water.

Landowners have waged a long battle with boaters about access to and use of the river. To avoid problems, stay the night before you put on at the campground at Baker's Crossing, get on the river early, and try to make it to Devils River State Natural Area (mile 15) for the first night.

In that stretch there is only one noteable drop at mile 10, a five-foot-high cut through a ledge that is split in the middle by an outcropped rooster tail. If you hang up on the rooster tail, you can wrap your boat. (I saw this happen to a seventeen-foot Coleman canoe. After freeing the boat, we tied a rope around it to hold the plastic against the broken aluminum frame and floated it down to the park. That night we duct-taped a branch to the aluminum frame as a splint for the rest of the trip.)

If you make arrangements beforehand, you can put on the river from the park early in the morning. Otherwise, the gate is

Threading Dolan Falls at low water. Photo by Shawn Hokanson

locked. You must have a State Park Conservation Pass ($50) and pay $25 to have your vehicle shuttled from the gate to the river. Fax inquiries to the park superintendent at (830) 395-2133.

Below Dolan Falls the flow picks up due to springs in the area. A few more rapids occur in the next ten miles, but then the run turns into a float trip through scenic canyons to the place where Lake Amistad backs up to Pafford Crossing (mile 34) northeast of Comstock. Nine miles of lake paddling get you from there to the marina.

Bill Leon and Steve Daniel at the Devils River's Dolan Falls. Photo by Shaun Hokanson

Rather than ruin your trip by fighting against winds that kick up on the lake, arrange for a motorboat pickup at Pafford as part of a package deal for shuttling your vehicles. That way you can relax, drink something cold, and be refreshed for your drive home. When the lake is low and motorboats cannot get to Pafford, most people arrange to be picked up just above the confluence of the Dry Devils River at Blue Sage Subdivision (mile 25). For information, contact Gerald Bailey at (830) 395-2266, High Bridge Adventures in Comstock at (915) 292-4495, or Rough Canyon Marina at (915) 775-8779.

As with the Lower Canyons of the Rio Grande, this is the kind of trip that is best thought of as an opportunity to be with friends in a remote environment, not a whitewater adventure.

For the latest flow information (updated every three hours), call the Del Rio IBWC office at (830) 775-2437 or the Hugheys at Baker's Crossing, at (915) 292-4503, for the Pafford Crossing flow. If you want a rough idea about flows when there is not any change in the weather, consult the IBWC Web site. It is updated on Monday and Thursday.

Appendix A
Sources of Water Level Information

HAVING UP-TO-DATE RIVER-FLOW DATA is crucial for anyone who paddles whitewater. In recent years the Internet has made access to that information much easier. Today serious paddlers have to be Internet literate if they expect to know when streams are running.

Because there is a bewildering assortment of flow information on the Net, most paddlers consult only a few sources and rely on what they know best. That means they seldom explore new streams and have no basis on which to judge when less frequently paddled creeks or rivers are runnable. My descriptions of each run and suggestions about minimum flow levels are intended to provide such a basis.

To indicate desirable water levels without explaining how to obtain information about them would hardly be helpful. Appendix B provides a table of river-flow gauge sites and lists sources of information.

Water Level Information Available on the Internet

Due to incompatible reporting mechanisms and conflicting policies of government agencies, you must consult a number of different sources to get Texas water-flow information. Although the situation seems to improve daily, the best information is available from Web sites (or URLs) maintained by the following:

- U.S. Geological Survey (USGS)
- Lower Colorado River Authority (LCRA)
- U.S. Army Corps of Engineers (C of E)
- International Boundary Waters Commission (IBWC)
- National Weather Service (NWS)

U.S. Geological Survey. By far the most comprehensive location for Texas riverflow information is the U.S. Geological Survey Web site:

http://txwww.cr.usgs.gov/cgi-bin/current/?sortby=basin&type=unit

This site is updated every few hours from numerous river gauging stations and provides historical flow-rate data and links to maps showing gauge locations. Streams are organized according to river basins. During major rainstorms the site may be slow or inaccessible. By omitting everything after "current/," you can obtain rainfall information.

Adrian Nye has created a reporting system that facilitates using the USGS gauge readings. You simply select specific streams and gauge levels, and the system automatically notifies you by e-mail when the streams reach their designated levels. Sign up for the service at

http://www.down-river.com/riverwatch/riverwatch.html

Nye's program is a wonderful example of how boaters can use their computer skills to take advantage of Internet information.

Some USGS gauges are not listed at the main USGS site but are accessible in another directory:

http://txwww.cr.usgs.gov/cgi-bin/uv_data/

This URL lists the codes you need to get specific information regarding gauges, data, and options for different time periods. To use this directory, you must know the number of the gauge station you are interested in. For a list of those numbers, check

http://txwww.cr.usgs.gov/current/docs/example.station.list.rdb

To determine, for example, the cfs flow on the Pecos River near Langtry (one of the USGS gauge sites not included in the "current" directory), add the following to the USGS URL, after "uv_data/":

?station=08447410&pmcode=00060&fmt=rdb&period=today

In this string

- the question mark indicates a query
- the station number is the Pecos gauge near Langtry
- the pmcode indicates the flow level
- the format (or fmt) "rdb" refers to a listing of hourly flows in tab-separated columns
- the period is the time span (e.g., since midnight).

By changing the codes you can get information on gauge height rather than cfs, or you can format your data in HTML rather than ASCII code.

As of October 1998, the USGS site lacks information from certain gauge stations maintained by the LCRA and the IBWC. Flow rates at some stations on the Colorado, Llano, Rio Grande, Pecos, and Devils Rivers are excluded.

Lower Colorado River Authority. For information on the Colorado River drainage, consult the Lower Colorado River Authority site at

http://www.lcra.org/water/gage.html

The site has five links of interest. The upper watershed page includes the upper Colorado River, San Saba River, Cherokee Creek, Llano River, Sandy Creek, and Pedernales River. The lower watershed page includes Bull, Barton, and Onion Creeks. The lake level page shows whether Lake Buchanan is full. The river report page indicates what is happening at Buchanan, Tom Miller, and Longhorn Dams. The rainfall data page reports hourly rainfall amounts.

The LCRA site is updated hourly; however, only the latest hour's flow is reported. Consequently, unless you check the site repeatedly, you cannot know whether the flow level is going up or down. To find out for reference purposes what the river level was at the put-on or take-out time, call LCRA at (800) 776-LCRA and request that information from their database.

U.S. Army Corps of Engineers. The Fort Worth office of the Corps of Engineers maintains a Web site with dam release information. This is especially useful if you want to take advantage of play spots below the dams or to see whether water is going over spillways. The address is

http://swf66.swf-wc.usace.army.mil

International Boundary Waters Commission. The IBWC posts gauge information for the Rio Grande, Devils, and Pecos Rivers on Mondays and Thursdays at

http://www.ibwc.state.gov/flowdata.htm

Although this information can hardly be considered timely, it is adequate for most boaters since these runs are generally multi-day affairs involving advanced planning. For current data on these rivers, consult other sites or telephone the numbers referenced in the river descriptions.

National Weather Service. The National Weather Service compiles data in files (or "products") that are usually available for in-house use only, especially by the NWS's River Forecast Centers. Most of the information, though, is accessible at the USGS site. Some gauge stations or Data Collection Platforms (DCPs) are not on the USGS list but are included in other NWS products listed in appendix B.

Archive Sites. Information from the USGS, the LCRA, and the Corps of Engineers are combined in data archives stored at a number of places around the nation. One of the most complete (though not necessarily the most user-friendly) site is at the University of Kentucky:

gopher://shelley.ca.uky.edu:70/00/.agwx/usr/public/

To get information about flows on a number of Texas streams at this site, add one of the following specific NWS file names to the end of this address.

FTWRVAFTW (for North Texas)
SATRVASAT (for South Texas)
LBBRVALBB (for West Texas)
LBBRVASJT (for Central Texas)

These files have the same information but different names at other Web sites. Although not all NWS files are available at all Web sites, the archives at Ohio State University, the University of North Carolina–Charlotte, and Florida State University are among the best. Their root addresses are

gopher://twister.sbs.ohio-state.edu:70/0/wxascii/rivercond/
http://asp1.sbs.ohio-state.edu/text/wxascii/rivercond/
http://ws321.uncc.edu/data/raw/RWUS/
http://www.met.fsu.edu/weather/

The endings you have to add to the Ohio State addresses after the slash are slightly different from those at the Kentucky site. They include

riverUS11.KFTW (for North Texas)
riverUS11.KSAT (for South Texas)
riverUS22.KFTW (for weekend dam releases and West Texas rivers)

The University of North Carolina/Charlotte and Florida State University sites are also organized differently, and files are arranged in subdirectories (e.g., RWUS11). The US22 file provides predicted releases and flows on the Frio, Guadalupe, Llano, Pedernales, San Marcos, Rio Grande, and Pecos Rivers based on observations at 6 A.M. on Wednesday. Any significant rainfall after Wednesday can make those predictions meaningless.

If you need to check Fort Worth (FTW) and San Antonio (SAT) files, you can see both together at

http://iwin.nws.noaa.gov/iwin/tx/hydro.html

If you have difficulty accessing archive sites, or if the information is dated, peer into the in-house files of the Lubbock NWS office, whose root address is

http://dryline.nws.noaa.gov/other_afos_data/NMC/RRA

For Rio Grande, Pecos, San Saba, or Llano River flows, always check the University of Kentucky site or elsewhere before consulting the Lubbock NWS computer. The "dryline" computer is not designed to handle heavy traffic, so use it only when everything else fails. Otherwise, the Lubbock office will be forced to close down public access to this rare and valuable resource. However, if you cannot get the information elsewhere, access it by adding one of the following to the Lubbock (dryline) root address:

LBBRVALBB (for West Texas)
LBBRVASJT (for Central Texas)

All the files or products mentioned so far can be read without any particular guide to decipher the three-letter DCP identification codes. Other useful files, updated every six hours from data collection sites around the state, refer to those codes and are available only through the Lubbock NWS computer.

LBBRVATX1 (for East Texas)
LBBRVATX2 (for Central Texas)
LBBRVATX3 (for West Texas)

During significant weather events a file may be updated more frequently to provide data from a particular station. In that case most of the other stations will not appear on the list or will not have any values assigned to them.

The table in appendix B provides the DCPs that you need to interpret the data from the files. Each line indicates rainfall and water level. For example,

PDAT2 DH1230/.00/23.97/1.54/
TELT2 DH1230/.00/8.46/3.78/

means that at 12:30 P.M. (Greenwich Mean Time, usually six hours ahead of Texas), the Pecos at Pandale was at 1.54 feet, the Rio Grande at Johnson Ranch upstream from Mariscal Canyon was at 3.78 feet, and no rain had fallen at either gauge in the previous six hours. (The 23.97 and 8.46 figures refer to total accumulated rainfall since the gauge was last reset; any numbers after the last slash refer to the pool elevation of a lake.) Although the information is generally listed this way, sometimes the order is changed. It helps to know an approximate range of figures you are seeking.

National Weather Service Flood Warnings. Local television stations commonly post flood warnings issued by the National Weather Service. Such warnings can be found at the NWS Flash Flood Warnings site:

http://iwin.nws.noaa.gov/iwin/tx/flashflood.html

Most flood warnings are arranged by county. Table 1 indicates by county the streams that can be affected by heavy rain. Because large rivers (e.g., the Trinity, Brazos, and Colorado) are dam-controlled, they are usually less sensitive to flood runoff than their tributaries. But after heavy rains, dam releases often increase flow for days, so it's helpful to know some of the counties included in the watersheds of those rivers.

TABLE 1

STREAMS TO CHECK AFTER HEAVY RAINS AND FLASH FLOODING

County	Stream	County	Stream
Bandera	Hondo Creek Medina River Sabinal River San Geronimo Creek Verde Creek	Burnet	Cow Creek Rocky Creek San Gabriel River San Gabriel River, North Fork San Gabriel River, South Fork
Bell	Rocky Creek Salado Creek	Caldwell	San Marcos River
Bexar	Cibolo Creek San Geronimo Creek	Collin	Spring Creek White Rock Creek
Blanco	Blanco River North Grape Creek Pedernales River	Comal	Cibolo Creek Upper Guadalupe River
Bosque	Childress Creek Hog Creek Meridian Creek Neils Creek North Bosque River Steele Creek	Coryell	Bee House Creek Cowhouse Creek Hog Creek
Brewster	Rio Grande Terlingua Creek	Crockett	Pecos River
Brown	Colorado River near Bend	Dallas	Duck Creek Spring Creek White Rock Creek

TABLE 1 (continued)

County	Stream	County	Stream
Denton	Denton Creek	Kerr	Guadalupe River
Edwards	Hackberry Creek–Nueces River	Kimble	James River Johnson Fork, Llano River South Llano River Upper Llano River
Ellis	South Prong of Waxahachie Creek	Lampasas	Lampasas River
Erath	North Bosque River Paluxy River	Llano	Lower Llano River Sandy Creek
Fisher	Brazos River, Clear Fork	Mason	Beaver Creek James River Llano River
Gillespie	Crabapple Creek North Grape Creek Pedernales River	McCulloch	San Saba River
Guadalupe	San Marcos River	McLennan	Hog Creek Middle Bosque River Tonkawa Creek
Hamilton	Cowhouse Creek Lampasas River Meridian Creek Neils Creek North Bosque River	Medina	Hondo Creek San Geronimo Creek Verde Creek
Hays	Barton Creek Blanco River Onion Creek San Marcos River	Mills	Colorado River near Bend Lampasas River
Hill	Nolan River	Parker	Trinity River, Clear Fork
Hood	Paluxy River	Pecos	Pecos River
Johnson	Nolan River	Presidio	Alamito Creek Rio Grande
Jones	Brazos River, Clear Fork	Real	Dry Frio River Frio River
Kendall	Blanco River Cibolo Creek Guadalupe River Little Blanco River	San Saba	Cherokee Creek Colorado River near Bend San Saba River

TABLE 1 (continued)

Somervell	Paluxy River	Uvalde	Dry Frio River Frio River
Tarrant	Johnson Creek Trinity River, West Fork	Val Verde	Devils River Pecos River

Terrell	Pecos River	Williamson	Berry Creek
			Brushy Creek
			Salado Creek
			San Gabriel River
			San Gabriel River,
			  North Fork
			San Gabriel River,
			  South Fork

Travis	Barton Creek Bull Creek Colorado River Dams: Longhorn and Tom Miller Cow Creek Onion Creek Shoal Creek	Wise	Trinity River, West Fork

Radar Sites. Hundreds of sources on the Internet complement the Weather Channel and provide radar graphics, rainfall amounts, and forecasts that paddlers use to identify streams that might come up. The following radar sites help in anticipating exactly where the creeks might rise:

Austin

http://www.austin360.com/cgi-bin/kvue/doppler.time.cgi
http://www.kxan.com/weather_images.html

San Antonio

http://www.intellicast.com/weather/sat/nexrad/
http://www.weather.com/weather/radar/single_site/TX_San_Antonio.html

Dallas–Fort Worth

http://www.kxas.com/radar2.shtml
http://www.intellicast.com/weather/dfw/radar/

San Angelo

http://www.intellicast.com/weather/sjt/nexrad/

If you are curious about watershed boundaries, consult the following site for maps of more than 200 streams in the state:

http://www.epa.gov/cgi-bin/surf/search.pl?geography=state&value=TX

Private Sources. Desert Sports provides information on Rio Grande flows in Big Bend Monday through Friday on its Web page:

http://www.desertsportstx.com/DS/BBdaily.html

On weekends, call Desert Sports at (888) 989-6900, Outback Expeditions at (800) 343-1640, Big Bend River Tours at (800) 545-4240, Texas River Expeditions at (800) 839-7238, or Far Flung Adventures in Terlingua at (800) 359-4138.

Newsgroups. Most canoe clubs and organizations in the state have their own home pages (often with pictures) with links to river and weather information. Newsgroups such as rec.boats.paddle can serve as an initial source for making contacts with boaters in the state and elsewhere. For those who want to see what Texas paddlers are talking about, canoeTX@world.std.com is probably the most common online discussion group. To subscribe to this group, send an untitled message to canoeTX-request@world.std.com with the text message "subscribe" (without the quotation marks).

Clubs and Organizations

A number of Texas paddling clubs and organizations have members whose interest is primarily whitewater. For basic river and organizational skills, you might contact paddlers affiliated with the American Canoe Association. Whitewater enthusiasts, however, often learn their skills from boaters who avoid local clubs and monthly meetings, although they may join American Whitewater (formerly the American Whitewater Affiliation) to receive the magazine *American Whitewater.*

To find those who paddle more difficult whitewater, you may have to forego the club scene and simply show up at a put-in after a heavy rain.

In the meantime, getting in touch with the following groups may help you locate someone other than outdoor-shop employees, raft guides, or club social coordinators to tell you about whitewater opportunities in the state.

Alamo City Rivermen
P.O. Box 171194
San Antonio, TX 78217-1194
Nancy Burns, (210) 641-8174 or
David Reichert, (210) 545-0548
reichert@world.std.com

Austin Paddling Club
P.O. Box 14211
Austin, TX 78761-4211
Paula Scotney-Castle
(512) 448-5171 or 292-3783
scotney@io.com
www.io.com/~apc

Bayou City Whitewater Club
P.O. Box 980782
Houston, TX 77098-0782
Scott Coultas, (281) 843-2971
www.bcwc.net

Big Thicket Voyageurs Canoe &
    Kayak Club
P.O. Box 787
Sour Lake, TX 77659-0787
Sandra Laurents, (409) 287-2210
BTVCanoe@aol.com
members.aol.com/btvcanoe/

Dallas DownRiver Club
P.O. Box 820246
Dallas, TX 75382-0246
Rich Grayson
214-827-0144
www.down-river.com

Georgetown Canoe & Kayak Club
121 Blue Quail
Georgetown, TX 78728
Paulo Pinto, (512) 863-8634

Hill Country Paddlers
P.O. Box 2301
Kerrville, TX 78029-2301
Bob Williams, (830) 896-3624,
Michael Van Winkle
830-895-2359
padwwmvw@hctc.com, or
Ron Duke 830-238-4400
mntsport@hctc.net
www.sig.net/~mtnsport/news.
    html

Houston Canoe Club
P.O. Box 925516
Houston, TX 77292-5516
713-467-8857
ruf.rice.edu/~pmontgom/canoe/
    HCC1.html

North Texas River Runners
P.O. Box 1152
Arlington, TX 76004-1152
Janet Lafferty 972-329-0642
janet138@swbell.net

Southwestern Whitewater Club
P.O. Box 120055
San Antonio, TX 78212
Bruce Walker
210-735-7970
lonestar.texas.net/~canoes/

Texas River Recreation
    Association
David Reichert
2622 Moss Bluff
San Antonio, TX 78232
210-545-0548
reichert@world.std.com
world.std.com/~reichert/canoeTX.
    htm

Appendix B
Stream Flow Data Locations

FOR INFORMATION ON ACCESSING Internet Web sites listed in the following table, consult appendix A. In this table

- USGS refers to the USGS Web site
- LCRA refers to the LCRA Web site
- C of E refers to the Corps of Engineers Web site
- IBWC refers to the International Boundary Waters Commission Web site
- US11FTW includes riverUS11.KFTW and FTWRVAFTW files
- US11SAT includes riverUS11.KSAT and SATRVASAT files
- LBBLBB refers to the LBBRVALBB file
- LBBSJT refers to the LBBRVASJT file
- TX1 refers to the LBBRVATX1 file
- TX2 refers to the LBBRVATX2 file
- TX3 refers to the LBBRVATX3 file
- NWS DCP IDs refers to National Weather Service Data Collection Platform three-letter identification codes

TABLE 2

STREAM FLOW DATA LOCATIONS

| Stream flow (✔) or dam release (X) | USGS | LCRA | C of E | IBWC | National Weather Service | | | | | | | NWS DCP IDs |
					US11 FTW	US11 SAT	LBB LBB	LBB SJT	TX 1	TX 2	TX 3	
Alamito Creek Rio Grande, Presidio Rio Grande, 5 mi SE of Presidio				✔			✔ ✔			✔	✔ ✔	PRD PRS
Barton Creek at Loop 360	✔	✔								✔		ABT
Beaver Creek	✔							✔				MBC
Bee House Creek Cowhouse Creek	✔				✔				✔			PIC

TABLE 2 (continued)

Stream flow (✔) or dam release (X)	USGS	LCRA	C of E	IBWC	US11 FTW	US11 SAT	LBB LBB	LBB SJT	TX 1	TX 2	TX 3	NWS DCP IDs
Berry Creek	✔					✔				✔		GTW
Blanco River	✔					✔				✔		WMB
Brazos River 　Clear Fork	✔							✔				NGT
Brazos River 　Hidalgo Falls 　Lake Somerville	✔		X							✔		BBZ SOM
Brazos River 　Port Sullivan	✔									✔		BBZ
Bull Creek	✔	✔								✔		ABU
Brushy Creek 　San Gabriel, 　　South Fork 　Berry Creek 　Bull Creek	✔ ✔ ✔	✔				✔				✔ ✔ ✔		GET GTW ABU
Cherokee Creek		✔										CKC
Childress Creek 　Hog Creek	✔				✔				✔			CRF
Cibolo Creek at Selma Cibolo Creek at 　Boerne	✔ ✔									✔		SEL BRN
Colorado River at Bend 　Red Bluff/San Saba	✔	✔			✔			✔			✔	SNB
Colorado River: 　Lake Buchanan		X	X			X						BUD
Colorado River: 　Longhorn Dam 　Tom Miller Dam, 　Lake Austin		X				X						ASN ALK
Cow Creek 　San Gabriel River, 　　South Fork	✔					✔				✔		GET
Cowhouse Creek	✔				✔				✔			PIC

TABLE 2 (continued)

Stream flow (✔) or dam release (X)	USGS	LCRA	C of E	IBWC	US11 FTW	US11 SAT	LBB LBB	LBB SJT	TX 1	TX 2	TX 3	NWS DCP IDs
Crabapple Creek Sandy Creek Pedernales River	✔	✔ ✔				✔						KNL JOC
Denton Creek Lake Grapevine			X		X				X			GPV
Devils River				✔							✔	CMK
Dry Frio River Frio below Dry Frio	✔ ✔									✔ ✔		RWD UDE
Duck Creek Rowlett Creek	✔											SHC
Frio River	✔									✔		CNC
Guadalupe River Lower, at Sattler Canyon Dam	✔		X			X				✔		STL SMC
Guadalupe River Upper	✔					✔				✔		SRG
Hackberry Creek Nueces River at Laguna Frio River	✔ ✔									✔ ✔		UVA CNC
Hondo Creek Tarpley Kings Waterhole	✔ ✔									✔ ✔		TPH KWH
Hog Creek	✔				✔				✔			CRF
James River Llano at Mason Llano at Junction		✔ ✔				✔ ✔		✔ ✔				MLR JNC
Johnson Creek Arlington rain gauge									X			LAR
Johnson Fork of the Llano River Llano at Junction		✔				✔		✔				JNC
Lampasas River	✔				✔				✔			KEM

TABLE 2 (continued)

Stream flow (✔) or dam release (X)	USGS	LCRA	C of E	IBWC	National Weather Service							NWS DCP IDs
					US11 FTW	US11 SAT	LBB LBB	LBB SJT	TX 1	TX 2	TX 3	
Llano River, Lower Llano at Mason Llano at Llano	 ✔	 ✔ ✔				 ✔ ✔	 	 ✔ 				 MLR LLA
Llano River, Upper Llano at Junction		✔				✔		✔				JNC
Llano River South Fork Llano at Junction		✔				✔		✔				JNC
Little Blanco River	✔					✔				✔		WMB
Medina River	✔									✔		BDA
Meridian Creek North Bosque at Clifton	✔				✔				✔			CTN
Middle Bosque River	✔				✔				✔			MCG
Neils Creek North Bosque at Clifton	✔				✔				✔			CTN
Nolan River	✔				✔				✔			BUM
North Bosque River North Bosque at Hico	✔				✔				✔			HIC
North Grape Creek Pedernales River	✔	✔				✔						JOC
Onion Creek near Driftwood at US 183	✔ ✔	 ✔								✔ 		DRW ATI
Paluxy River	✔				✔				✔			GRO
Pecos River Pandale Langtry				 ✔				✔ 		✔ ✔	✔	PDA LTR
Pedernales River	✔	✔				✔						JOC
Rio Grande Presidio Johnson's Ranch Rio Grande Village				 ✔ ✔				 ✔ ✔ ✔		 ✔ ✔	 ✔ ✔	PRD TEL RGV

TABLE 2 (continued)

Stream flow (✔) or dam release (X)	USGS	LCRA	C of E	IBWC	National Weather Service							NWS DCP IDs
					US11 FTW	US11 SAT	LBB LBB	LBB SJT	TX 1	TX 2	TX 3	
Rocky Creek Rocky Creek, South Fork	✔											BSJ
Sabinal River	✔									✔		SAB
Salado Creek Berry Creek	✔					✔				✔		GTW
San Gabriel River North Fork South Fork Berry Creek	✔ ✔ ✔					 ✔ ✔				✔ ✔ ✔		GER GET GTW
San Gabriel River, North Fork South Fork Lake Georgetown	✔ ✔ 		 X			 ✔ X				✔ ✔ X		GER GET GGL
San Gabriel River, South Fork	✔					✔				✔		GET
San Geronimo Creek Cibolo Creek at Boerne	✔									✔		BRN
San Marcos River	✔									✔		SRU
San Saba River Brady Menard San Saba		✔ ✔ ✔			✔ ✔ ✔			✔ ✔ ✔				BSS MNR SSB
Sandy Creek		✔										KNL
Shoal Creek	✔									✔		AHO
South Prong of Waxahachie Creek Mountain Creek	✔								✔			VNS
Spring Creek Rowlett Creek	✔											SHC
Steele Creek Paluxy River	✔				✔				✔			GRO
Terlingua Creek Rio Grande at Lajitas, Castolon							✔					(none)

TABLE 2 (continued)

Stream flow (✔) or dam release (X)	USGS	LCRA	C of E	IBWC	National Weather Service							NWS DCP IDs
					US11 FTW	US11 SAT	LBB LBB	LBB SJT	TX 1	TX 2	TX 3	
Tonkawa Creek 　Middle Bosque River	✔				✔				✔			MCG
Trinity River 　Clear Fork 　Lake Benbrook	✔		X		✔ X				✔			FWH BNB
Trinity River 　West Fork 　Lake Worth	✔		X		✔				✔ X			FWO FLW
Verde Creek 　Hondo Creek	✔									✔		KWH
White Rock Creek	✔											DWR

Appendix C
Overview of Legal Issues

IT WOULD BE NICE NOT TO HAVE TO DEAL with man-made barriers on navigable streams (especially since such barriers are illegal because they prevent citizens from using state property). But some landowners simply don't want us there at all. So after telling us about the fence or dam, they think that they have done their duty and call for our arrest at the portage. They generally seem unphased by the prospect that they will be forced to remove an obstacle if a stream is declared navigable.

If landowners were confident that all recreational users would not cut fences or leave trash, they would probably be more inclined to work with (rather than against) boaters. But they fear that the litter and drunken disregard of property that they see on streams like the Guadalupe below Canyon Dam will appear on their property.

Not surprisingly, some landowners would prefer not to have "their" streams identified as navigable. In fact, the head of one Texas landowners group recently asked the Texas Attorney General's (AG) office to create a list of streams and stream segments that are navigable in hopes that any unlisted stream would thereby be deemed non-navigable. That would mean that the burden of proof about the navigability of an unlisted stream would probably fall on the boater. Thankfully, the AG's office has ignored this request so far. But it is not inconceivable that the state legislature could decide to pass a law that would restrict citizen access to public resources in just this way.

With such a threat looming over them, some paddlers have decided that the safest response in the situation is to allay landowner fears by keeping certain runs secret. My own preference, acquired from boaters in the Southeast and in Colorado, is to spread the word about good runs while emphasizing the need to know the law and respect property rights.

The following summary of the legal background regarding access questions is by Joe Riddell, assistant Texas attorney general. Note that this summary is not a formal opinion of the AG's office, nor is it endorsed by the AG.

Even if you think that the law as summarized below supports your right to paddle a stream, that does not mean you will not be hassled, threatened, or arrested. Any judicial decision or declaratory judgment about a run's navigability can be contentious, expensive, and lengthy. So if you are going to take on a group of wealthy landowners to get access to a creek, make sure you have a boater-attorney to defend you who will work pro bono.

Overview of Laws Regarding the Navigation of Texas Streams, with Selected References to Statutes, Cases, and Other Materials

Presented to the Texas Rivers Conservation Advisory Board of the Texas
Parks and Wildlife Department
April 18, 1997

Compiled by Joe Riddell
Assistant Attorney General
Natural Resources Division, Office of the Attorney General of Texas

Opinions expressed in this paper do not necessarily reflect the opinions of the
Office of the Attorney General of Texas

Table of Contents

The Navigation Right

The navigation right encompasses a right of free passage along a river or stream. Long ago the Texas Supreme Court stated:

> [It has been] the settled policy and cherished object of the state to guard its navigable streams from obstruction and to secure and improve them as common highways of trade and travel for such of its citizens as might wish to use them for this purpose. *Selman* v. *Wolfe*, 27 Tex. 68, 71 (1863).

The navigation of Texas's inland and coastal waters is one of several "public rights and duties" specifically recognized by the Texas Constitution. A form of the right to travel, the navigation right is part of the liberty and the freedom of movement enjoyed by our society. Texas' laws on navigation have evolved under different governments during Texas' history. The laws are a blend of the civil law (the law of Spain and Mexico and the early Republic of Texas, which still applies to old land grants), the common law (court rulings), and statutes (acts of the Texas Legislature or the Congress of the Republic of Texas).

≈ ≈ ≈ ≈ ≈

Civil Law—from the *Partidas* (title 28 of third Partida), as translated in Frederic Hall, *The Laws of Mexico* (1885) pp. 447–49:

Law 3. *What are the Things Which Belong in Common to All Creatures Living.*
—The things which belong in common to all the living creatures of the world are the air, rain, water, the sea, and its shores; for every living creature may use them, according to his wants.

Law 6. *That Every One may Make Use of Ports, Rivers, and Public Roads.*
Rivers, ports, and public roads belong to all men in common; so that strangers

coming from foreign countries may make use of them, in the same manner as the inhabitants of the place where they are. And though the dominion or property (senorio) of the banks of rivers belongs to the owner of the adjoining estate, nevertheless, every man may make use of them to fasten his vessel to the trees that grow there, or to refit his vessel, or to put his sails or merchandise there. So fishermen may put and expose their fish for sale there, and dry their nets, or make use of the banks for all like purposes, which appertain to the art or trade by which they live.

Law 8. That No One has a Right to Build a Mill or Other Edifice on a River, by Which the Navigation of Vessels may be Obstructed.—No man has a right to dig a new canal, construct a new mill, house, tower, cabin, or any other building whatever, in rivers which are navigated by vessels, nor upon their banks, by which the common use of them may be obstructed. And if he does, whether the canal or edifice be newly or anciently made, if it interfere with such common use, it ought to be destroyed. For it is not just that the common good of all men generally should be sacrificed to the interest of some persons only.

Concerning the civil law, Joaquin Escriche, *Diccionario Razonado de Legislación y Jurisprudencia* (1831), as translated in Hall, *The Laws of Mexico* (1885) pp. 411, 416–17, states:

Public Waters.—Waters which are not nor can not be private property belong to the public. Such are the waters of the rivers which by themselves or by accession with others follow their course to the sea. These may be navigable or not navigable. If they are navigable, nobody can avail himself of them so as to hinder or embarrass navigation.

River, What is—Uses thereof—Their banks.—A river is a mass of water united between two banks, which run perpetually from time immemorial. It differs from a torrent in that this is the effect of the abundant rains or extraordinary meltings of snow, so that it runs only a certain time and leaves its bed dry the greater part of the year. Rivers, as law 6, title 28, partidas 3, says, belong to all men generally so that even those who are of other foreign lands may use them as the natives and residents of the territory which they bathe. . . . [A]nd when a river which is not navigable becomes so after uniting with another, use of its waters must be made so that then there shall be no lack thereof for navigation.

Texas Constitution, Art. XVI, § 59 ("The Conservation Amendment"):

(a) The conservation and development of all of the natural resources of this State. . . , the conservation and development of its forests, water, and hydro-electric power, the navigation of its inland and coastal waters, and the preservation and conservation of all such natural resources of the State are each and all hereby declared public rights and duties; and the Legislature shall pass all such laws as may be appropriate thereto.

General discussions, with citations to many cases about navigable streams, are found in the following legal treatises:

Texas Jurisprudence, 3rd ed, vol. 73, *Water* (1990), esp. §§ 204–48; and Wells A. Hutchins, *The Texas Law of Water Rights* (1961).

Regarding the civil law, see also Betty E. Dobkins, *The Spanish Element in Texas Water Law* (1959).

Regarding freedom of movement, see Zechariah Chafee, *Three Human Rights in the Constitution of 1787* (1956).

Navigability

In Texas a stream is navigable if it is either "navigable in fact" or "navigable by statute." These tests are explained below. Simply put, a non-navigable stream is a stream that is neither navigable in fact nor navigable by statute. Along a navigable stream, the public may boat, fish, swim, camp, and in general carry on any legal activity. Public use must be confined to the streambed and, to a limited extent, the banks.

Along a non-navigable stream, the public generally has no right of use, and a private landowner may forbid public entry upon or along the waterway. However, there are some instances in which a perennial stream, even though it is not navigable in fact or navigable by statute, is nevertheless open to public use because the land bordering it was granted (prior to December 14, 1837) under the civil law, which reserved ownership of beds of perennial streams to the sovereign.

Navigable in Fact

A number of criteria have been suggested for whether a stream is navigable in fact. Some relate to passage by boats, others to the ability to float logs, and still others to a stream's usefulness in commerce. Various courts, both state and federal, have recognized different tests. Texas courts have acknowledged a wide range of uses in support of navigability in fact.

≈ ≈ ≈ ≈ ≈

Tests for Navigability in Fact

Texas courts have sometimes found navigability as a result of capacity for commercial use. See, e.g., *Jones* v. *Johnson*, 25 S.W. 650, 651 (Tex.Civ.App. 1894, writ ref'd) and *Orange Lumber Co.* v. *Thompson*, 126 S.W. 604, 606 (Tex.Civ.App. 1910, no writ). The Texas Supreme Court in *Selman* v. *Wolfe*, 27 Tex. 68, 71 (1863) (quoted above, p. 171) has recognized a broad concept for navigable streams—that of "common highways of trade and travel."

The case of *Welder* v. *State*, 196 S.W. 868, 873 (Tex.Civ.App.— Austin 1917, writ ref'd) has discussed the concept underlying the "navigable in fact" tests:

Behind all definitions of navigable waters lies the idea of public utility. Waters which in their natural state are useful to the public for a considerable portion of the year are navigable. Boats are mentioned in the decisions because boats are the usual means by which waters are utilized by the public, and commerce is usually mentioned because carrying produce and merchandise is the usual public demand for such waters. But floating logs has frequently been held to be navigation, and hunting and fishing, and even pleasure boating, ha[ve] been held to be proper public uses. See also 73 Tex. Jur. 3d *Water* § 209 (1990).

The federal power over navigable streams derives from the federal government's powers over interstate commerce set out in the U.S. Constitution. Thus, the federal test of navigability in fact relates to use as highways for commerce. States are free to adopt, and most have adopted, broader concepts of navigability for the purposes of state regulation. (Of course, state control of waters is subject to federal jurisdiction for interstate commerce and navigation.)

Navigable by Statute

Under a law dating from 1837, a stream is navigable so far as it retains an average width of thirty feet from its mouth up. The width measured is the distance between the fast (or firmly fixed) land banks. A stream satisfying the thirty-foot rule is sometimes referred to as "statutorily navigable" or "navigable by statute." Under a court decision, the public has rights along a stream navigable by statute just as if the stream were navigable in fact.

≈ ≈ ≈ ≈ ≈

Original Statutory Provision (effective December 14, 1837):

> That all streams of the average width of 30 feet shall be considered navigable streams within the meaning of this act, so far up as they retain that average width, and that they shall not be crossed by the lines of a survey. Sayles' *Early Laws of Texas*, p. 271, quoted at 286 S.W. 466.

Current Statutes

Natural Resources Code § 21.001. Definitions:

> In this chapter. . . (c) "Navigable stream" means a stream which retains an average width of 30 feet from the mouth up.

Natural Resources Code § 21.012. Surveys on Navigable Streams:

> (a) If the circumstances of the lines previously surveyed under the law will permit, land surveyed for individuals, lying on a navigable stream, shall front one-half of the square on the stream with the line running at right angles with the general course of the stream.
> (b) A navigable stream may not be crossed by the lines of a survey.

Diversion Lake Club v. *Heath*, 126 Tex. 129, 86 S.W.2d 441, 445 (1935):

> Thus it is apparent that statutory navigable streams in Texas are public streams, and that their beds and waters are owned by the state in trust for the benefit and best interests of all the people, and subject to use by the public for navigation, fishing, and other lawful purposes, as fully and to the same extent that the beds and waters of streams navigable in fact are so owned and so held in trust and subject to such use.

Measurement of Stream Width for Navigability by Statute

The entire bed is to be included in the width, not just the area covered by flowing water. The bed extends all the way between the fast land banks. These are the banks that separate the streambed from the adjacent upland (whether valley or hill) and confine the waters to a definite channel. Further, stream segments having a width of less than thirty feet do not defeat the stream's navigability by statute, so long as the stream's width maintains an average of thirty feet or more.

≈ ≈ ≈ ≈ ≈

In *Motl* v. *Boyd*, 116 Tex. 82, 286 S.W. 458, 467 (1926), the Texas Supreme Court explained what a stream consists of:

> A water course, river, or stream consists of a bed, banks, and a stream of water. . . . The bed of a stream is that portion of its soil which is alternatively covered and left bare as there may be an increase or diminution in the supply of water, and which is adequate to contain it at its average and mean stage during an entire year, without reference to the extra freshets of the winter or spring or the extreme drouths of the summer or autumn. . . .The banks of a stream or river are the water-washed and relatively permanent elevations or acclivities at the outer lines of the river bed which separate the bed from the adjacent upland, whether valley or hill, and serve to confine the waters within the bed and preserve the course of the river when they rise to the highest point at which they are still confined to a definite channel.

> Since the stream is a navigable one, the elevations of land adjacent to its bed, which hold its navigable waters in place, and to which boats might be tied or anchored, and wharves or other instrumentalities of navigation attached, are its banks.

The court went on to explain the streambed measurement:

> [T]he bed of the stream defined by the statute is that portion of the terrain between its fast land banks. So when the statute says that the average width shall be 30 feet between the banks, it does not mean the space covered by the water at low tide or flow, but the entire bed of the stream as above defined.

In this case the court held that the creek involved was navigable by statute. It stated,

"The bed of the creek has an average width of more than 30 feet, although the waters flow in an ordinary season over less than 30 feet of this width." The court went on to note:

> The fact that at times and places there may be some distance between the bordering banks which limit the survey lines and the water does not militate against the right of the riparian owner to have access to the water. *Motl* v. *Boyd*, 116 Tex. 82, 286 S.W. 458, 468 (1926).

In a case involving the North Fork of the Guadalupe River, a question was raised because the stream was measured to be less than thirty feet wide for a short reach just above its mouth before it became substantially wider farther upstream. The court stated:

> Several witnesses testified as to the width of the river and the general import of their testimony is that the width of the river substantially exceeds thirty feet. Appellants' main complaint is with the method of measurement used. The statute provides no precise method of measurement for determining if a stream maintains an average width of thirty feet from the mouth up. We have found no case which absolutely mandates any certain method be used. We have concluded that the testimony in the record sufficiently supports the trial court's finding as to navigability. *Adjudication of Upper Guadalupe Segment of Guadalupe River Basin*, 625 S.W.2d 353, 362-3 (Tex.Civ.App.—San Antonio 1981), *aff'd*, 642 S.W. 2d 438 (1982).

The question of navigability of a stream is ultimately to be decided by the courts. See *State* v. *Bradford*, 121 Tex. 515, 50 S.W. 2d 1065, 1070 (1932).

Navigability of Lakes

There are very few natural lakes in Texas. Some of the small natural ones have been held to be non-navigable and therefore subject to private ownership and control. The typical Texas lake, on the other hand, has been created by building a dam on a navigable stream and then impounding water behind the dam. Damming a navigable stream does not destroy the public's navigation right along it. The Texas Supreme Court has held that persons may boat and fish on all the lake's waters, not just on the portion directly above the navigable stream. Therefore, a property owner may not fence off any portion of such a lake. The court also held that the public does not have a right to fish from the privately owned shores of an impoundment on a navigable stream. When a lake has been created by damming a non-navigable stream, the private landowner may (unless he holds under a civil law grant adjoining a perennial stream) prohibit public use of the lake—including boating and fishing.

≈ ≈ ≈ ≈ ≈

The effects upon public rights of damming a navigable stream were considered in a case involving the Medina River. In discussing the dam owner's permit, the Supreme Court stated:

It gave no title to the water, but only the right to divert and use so much of the water appropriated as might be necessarily required when beneficially used for the purpose for which it was appropriated. . . . It gave no title to the fish in the water of the lake, no exclusive right to take the fish from the lake, and no right to interfere with the public in their use of the river and its water for navigation, fishing, and other lawful purposes further than interference necessarily result[ing] from the construction and maintenance of the dams and lakes in such manner as reasonably to accomplish the purpose of the appropriation. *Diversion Lake Club* v. *Heath*, 126 Tex. 129, 86 S.W. 2d 441, 446 (1935).

The court held that persons may boat and fish on all of the lake's waters, not just on the portion directly above the navigable stream. As to fishing from the lake's shores, the court stated:

We find no authority for holding that the public have as an incident to the right to fish in Diversion Lake a right to use the banks of the lake, and it is our opinion that they have no such right. *Diversion Lake Club* v. *Heath*, 126 Tex. 129, 86 S.W. 2d 441, 447 (1935).

For a discussion of the private property rights associated with a non-navigable lake, see *Taylor Fishing Club* v. *Hammett*, 88 S.W. 2d 127 (Tex.Civ.App.—Waco 1935, writ dism'd).

Public Access to Navigable Streams

Access must usually be obtained through the use of public property. The typical access may be from the right-of-way of a public road that crosses the stream, through a publicly owned boat launch area, or from some other public land (a park, for example) adjacent to the stream. There is no general right to cross private property to get to a navigable stream. There are a number of privately owned parks or campgrounds where members of the public may have access to a navigable stream by paying a small fee to the landowner. If the private landowner forbids access, an attempt to use the private land is a trespass.

State law prohibits parking on a highway bridge and generally forbids (with certain exceptions) parking in the main traveled part of a highway.

Within a public road's right-of-way, private fencing that restricts public passage to the stream is illegal.

≈ ≈ ≈ ≈ ≈

Access via Public Road Crossing

Diversion Lake Club v. *Heath*, 126 Tex. 129, 86 S.W.2d 441, 442 (1935), explicitly recognized the legality of entering navigable waters from a public road:

Defendants . . . entered the waters of Diversion Lake and fished in it by placing their boats into the water from the low bridge on which the public road crosses the river and the lake near the upper end of the lake. Thus they were able to obtain access to the waters of the lake without trespassing upon the property of plaintiff.

Regarding parking, see the Texas Transportation Code, §§ 545.301–545.305.

Private Obstructions in a Public Road's Right-of-Way

In *Cornelison* v. *State*, 40 Tex. Crim. 159, 49 S.W. 384 (1899), a private party owned land on both sides of a thirty-foot wide roadway. A fourteen-foot-wide bridge spanned a creek. The landowner ran fences to the bridge corners, obstructing eight feet of right-of-way on each side of the bridge. The court upheld a criminal conviction of the landowner for obstructing a public road.

Today obstructing a highway or other passageway is a misdemeanor under Texas Penal Code § 42.03 (quoted below, pp. 183–84).

Regulation of Water Safety

After recognizing the navigation of Texas's inland and coastal waters to be a public right and duty, the Texas Constitution provides that the Texas Legislature "shall pass all such laws as may be appropriate thereto." The legislature has declared a policy of promoting the uniformity of laws relating to water safety. A number of such laws are contained in the Water Safety Act, Chapter 31 of the Texas Parks and Wildlife Code. The Water Safety Act applies to all public water of the state and to all watercraft navigated or moving on the public water. The basic authority for the enactment of boating regulations is reserved to the state; limited local regulations consistent with the Water Safety Act are permitted under Parks and Wildlife Code § 31.092. By special statute the legislature may also grant regulatory powers to a speci-fic authority.

≈ ≈ ≈ ≈ ≈

State Regulations

Chapter 31 of the Texas Parks and Wildlife Code has subchapters addressing general provisions, identification and numbering of vessels, titles for boats and motors, required equipment, boating regulations, enforcement and penalties, and boat ramps and buoys. Some provisions of note are the following:

Parks and Wildlife Code § 31.002. State Policy:

> It is the duty of this state to promote recreational water safety for persons and property in and connected with the use of all recreational water facilities in the state, to promote safety in the operation and equipment of facilities, and to promote uniformity of laws relating to water safety.

Parks and Wildlife Code § 31.022(c):

> All canoes, punts, rowboats, sailboats, and rubber rafts when paddled, poled, oared, or windblown are exempt from the numbering provisions of this chapter.

Parks and Wildlife Code § 31.073. Canoes, Punts, Rowboats, Sailboats, and Rubber Rafts; Equipment Exemptions:

> All canoes, punts, rowboats, sailboats, and rubber rafts when paddled, poled, oared, or windblown are exempt from all the required safety equipment except the following:
>> (1) one Coast Guard–approved lifesaving device for each person aboard; and
>> (2) the lights prescribed for class A vessels in Section 31.064 of this code.

Parks and Wildlife Code § 31.091. Uniformity of Boating Regulations:

> In the interest of uniformity, it is the policy of the State of Texas that the basic authority for the enactment of boating regulations is reserved to the state.

Parks and Wildlife Code § 31.093. Rules of the Road:

> The United States Coast Guard Inland Rules apply to all public water of this state to the extent they are applicable.

Parks and Wildlife Code § 31.096. Reckless Operation and Excessive Speed:

> No person may operate a vessel or manipulate water skis, an aquaplane, or a similar device on the water of this state in willful or wanton disregard of the rights or safety of others or without due caution or circumspection, and at a speed or in a manner that endangers, or is likely to endanger, a person or property.

Parks and Wildlife Code § 31.101. Obstructing Passage:

> (a) No person may anchor a boat in the traveled portion of a river or channel so as to prevent, impede, or interfere with the safe passage of any other boat through the same area.

> (b) No person may anchor a vessel near a state-owned boat ramp so as to prevent, impede, or interfere with the use of the boat ramp.

Parks and Wildlife Code § 31.102. Operating Boats in Restricted Areas:

> No person may operate a boat within a water area that has been clearly marked, by buoys or some other distinguishing device, as a bathing, fishing, swimming, or otherwise restricted area by the department or by a political subdivision of the state. This section does not apply to a patrol or rescue craft or in the case of an emergency.

Local Regulations

Parks and Wildlife Code § 31.092. Local Regulations:

(a) The governing body of an incorporated city or town, with respect to public water within its corporate limits and all lakes owned by it, may designate by ordinance certain areas as bathing, fishing, swimming, or otherwise restricted areas and may make rules and regulations relating to the operation and equipment of boats which it deems necessary for the public safety. The rules and regulations shall be consistent with the provisions of this chapter.

(b) The commissioners court of a county, with respect to public water within the territorial limits of the county that is outside of the limits of an incorporated city or town or a political subdivision designated in Subsection (c) of this section and that are not lakes owned by an incorporated city or town, may enter an order on its books designating certain areas as bathing, fishing, swimming, or otherwise restricted areas and may make rules and regulations relating to the operation and equipment of boats which it deems necessary for the public safety. The rules and regulations shall be consistent with the provisions of this chapter.

(c) The governing board of a political subdivision of the state created pursuant to Article XVI, Section 59, of the Texas Constitution, for the purpose of conserving and developing the public water of the state, with respect to public water impounded within lakes and reservoirs owned or operated by the political subdivision, may designate by resolution or other appropriate order certain areas as bathing, fishing, swimming, or otherwise restricted areas and may make rules and regulations relating to the operation and equipment of boats which it deems necessary for the public safety. The rules and regulations shall be consistent with the provisions of this chapter.

(d) A copy of all rules and regulations adopted under this section shall be summarily filed with the department.

(e) No city, town, village, special district, or other political subdivision of the state may impose or collect a fee for the registration or inspection of vessels to be used on public water against the owner or operator of a vessel used on public water. This section does not apply to Chapter 321, Tax Code, nor to any launch fees, docking fees, entry fees, or other recreational fees which may be imposed or collected by any political subdivision of the State of Texas for the use of the facilities afforded by any such district to the public.

The Water Oriented Recreation District of Comal County functions under Chapter 324 of the Texas Local Government Code. Section 324.066 provides in part:

(a) The board [of the district] may adopt reasonable rules and ordinances applicable to: . . .

(2) littering and litter abatement on the public water in the district, including the possession and disposition of glass containers;

(3) activities that endanger the health and safety of persons or property on public water in the district, subject to the public's paramount right to navigate inland water.

Lawful Activities along Navigable Streams

Texas courts have recognized that a member of the public may engage in a variety of lawful activities along a navigable stream. Besides boating, persons may swim, float, walk, wade, picnic, camp, and (with a license) fish. Public use must be confined to the streambed and, to a limited extent, the banks. Hunting is permitted in some situations. However, a hunter should always check first with local law enforcement officials because of numerous local restrictions and exceptions. A law called the Sportsman's Rights Act prohibits intentional interference with or disruption of lawful hunting or fishing.

In general, any unlawful activity is also unlawful along a river. The disorderly conduct provision of the Texas Penal Code forbids such activities as fighting, being unreasonably noisy, displaying a firearm in a manner calculated to alarm, discharging a firearm, and using abusive or profane language that tends to incite an immediate breach of peace. Damaging or destroying property is punished as criminal mischief. Under another law punishment for littering can range up to a fine of $4,000 and a year in jail, depending upon the amount of litter and any previous convictions.

≈ ≈ ≈ ≈ ≈

Lawful Activities

The case of *Dincans* v. *Keeran*, 192 S.W. 603 (Tex.Civ.App.—San Antonio 1917, no writ) recognized a public right to use the waters and shoreline. In overturning the lower court's decree for being too restrictive, the court stated:

> [T]he trial court's decree was too comprehensive [in that it] restrained appellants from the enjoyment of their lawful right to use the shore line of the navigable waters, which formed the western boundary of appellees' land. . . . Hunting, camping, and fishing are reasonable uses of the navigable waters and shore line.

Diversion Lake Club v. *Heath*, 126 Tex. 129, 86 S.W.2d 441, 445 (1935), stated:

> Thus it is apparent that statutory navigable streams in Texas are public streams, and that their beds and waters are owned by the state in trust for the benefit and best interests of all the people, and subject to use by the public for navigation, fishing, and other lawful purposes, as fully and to the same extent that the beds and waters of streams navigable in fact are so owned and so held in trust and subject to such use.

Texas Attorney General's Opinion S-208 (1956) concluded that the general public is authorized to walk down the dry or submerged bed of a navigable stream—

even if its bed is privately owned by virtue of the Small Bill (Art. 5414a, R.C.S.)—for the purpose of seining and fishing in water holes in the bed of the river. Such conduct was not a criminal trespass under the definition of the crime then in effect.

The Sportsman's Rights Act

Parks and Wildlife Code § 62.0125. Harassment of Hunters, Trappers, and Fishermen:

(a) This section may be cited as the Sportsman's Rights Act.

(b) In this section:

(1) "Wildlife" means all species of wild mammals, birds, fish, reptiles, or amphibians.

(2) "Process of hunting or catching" means any act directed at the lawful hunting or catching of wildlife, including camping or other acts preparatory to hunting or catching of wildlife that occur on land or water on which the affected person has the right or privilege of hunting or catching that wildlife.

(c) No person may intentionally interfere with another person lawfully engaged in the process of hunting or catching wildlife.

(d) No person may intentionally harass, drive, or disturb any wildlife for the purpose of disrupting a person lawfully engaged in the process of hunting or catching wildlife.

(e) No person may enter or remain on public land or enter or remain on private land without the landowner's or his agent's consent if the person intends to disrupt another person lawfully engaged in the process of hunting or catching wildlife.

(f) This section does not apply to a peace officer of this state, a law enforcement officer of the United States, a member of the armed forces of the United States or of this state, or employees of the department or other state or federal agencies having statutory responsibility to manage wildlife or land during the time that the officer is in the actual discharge of official duties.

(g) A person who violates this section commits an offense. An offense under this section is a Class B misdemeanor.

(h) It is an affirmative defense to prosecution that the defendant's conduct is protected by the right to freedom of speech under the constitution of this state or the United States.

Unlawful Conduct

See laws such as the following:
Texas Penal Code § 42.01, Disorderly Conduct
Texas Penal Code § 49.02, Public Intoxication
Texas Penal Code § 49.06, Boating While Intoxicated
Texas Penal Code § 28.03, Criminal Mischief
Texas Penal Code § 22.07, Terroristic Threat
Texas Health and Safety Code, Chapter 365, Texas Litter Abatement Act
Texas Parks & Wildlife Code, Chapters 61, 62, and 82, regarding fishing, hunting, and preserves

Private Uses, Obstructions, Bridges, and Dams

Since the days of the civil law of Spain and Mexico, obstructions of navigable streams have been forbidden. Nowadays the Texas Penal Code and the Texas Water Code forbid obstructions, and the Texas Natural Resources Code forbids unauthorized private structures. State officials may take actions to remove them. An obstruction may also be unlawful as a purpresture (a legal term for an encroachment upon public rights and easements or the appropriation to private use of that which belongs to the public). Likewise, an obstruction may be subject to removal as a public nuisance.

State laws do allow state officials to permit, under certain circumstances, private uses and bridges and dams. A permit is generally required from the Parks and Wildlife Commission for any disturbance or taking of marl, sand, gravel, shell, or mudshell. The Commissioner of the General Land Office has some authority to grant easements for rights of way across navigable or state-owned streambeds for such purposes as powerlines, pipelines, and roads. A permit from the Texas Natural Resource Conservation Commission is required before anyone may build a dam or otherwise store, take, or divert state water from a navigable stream. Even on a non-navigable stream, a permit is required for a dam impounding more than 200 acre-feet of water.

Obstructions

Civil Law (from Title 28 of the third Partida):

> Law 8. *That No One has a Right to Build a Mill or Other Edifice on a River, by Which the Navigation of Vessels may be Obstructed.*—No man has a right to dig a new canal, construct a new mill, house, tower, cabin, or any other building whatever, in rivers which are navigated by vessels, nor upon their banks, by which the common use of them may be obstructed. And if he does, whether the canal or edifice be newly or anciently made, if it interfere with such common use, it ought to be destroyed. For it is not just that the common good of all men generally should be sacrificed to the interest of some persons only.

Water Code § 11.096:

> No person may obstruct the navigation of any stream which can be navigated by steamboats, keelboats, or flatboats by cutting and felling trees or by building on or across the stream any dike, milldam, bridge, or other obstruction.

Penal Code § 42.03. Obstructing Highway or Other Passageway:

> (a) A person commits an offense if, without legal privilege or authority, he intentionally, knowingly, or recklessly . . . obstructs a highway, street, sidewalk, railway, waterway, elevator, aisle, hallway, entrance, or exit to which the public or a substantial group of the public has access, or any other place used for the passage of persons, vehicles, or conveyances, regardless of the means of creating

the obstruction and whether the obstruction arises from his acts alone or from his acts and the acts of others. . .

(b) For the purposes of this section, "obstruct" means to render impassable or to render passage unreasonably inconvenient or hazardous.

(c) An offense under this section is a Class B misdemeanor.

Purpresture

Purprestures were discussed in *Trice* v. *State*, 712 S.W. 2d 842 (Tex.App.—Waco 1986, writ ref'd n.r.e.), a case concerning a private bridge across the Brazos River. The court noted (at p. 849) that a purpresture "would be subject to be removed at the instance of the State, whether the same should tend to obstruct navigation or otherwise." The court, concluding that the private bridge was a purpresture because it encroached upon the state's land without its permission, ordered that the bridge be removed.

Nuisance

For an early case recognizing a private right to remove, as a nuisance, an unlawful obstruction to navigation, see *Selman* v. *Wolfe*, 27 Tex. 68 (1863).

Obstruction by Fencing

Texas Attorney General Opinion S-107 (1953) addressed fishing rights of the public along a stretch of the Trinity River bordered by Mexican land grants made under the civil law in 1835. The summary of the opinion stated:

> The public may use the bed and banks of the Trinity River up to the gradient boundary for fishing and may make certain uses of its banks above that line if they are held under civil law grants. The riparian owners cannot prevent the public from gaining access to the river by means of a highway right-of-way by erection of a fence thereon and cannot prevent the public from going up and down the river in boats and fishing in its waters by the erection of fences across the river.

Authority of Commissioner of General Land Office

Natural Resources Code § 51.291. Grants of Easements:

> (a) Except as provided by Subsection (b) of this section, the commissioner [of the General Land Office] may execute grants of easements for rights-of-way across, through, and under unsold public school land, the portion of the Gulf of Mexico within the jurisdiction of the state, the state-owned riverbeds and beds of navigable streams in the public domain, and all islands, saltwater lakes, bays, inlets, marshes, and reefs owned by the state within tidewater limits for:
>   (1) telephone, telegraph, electric transmission, and powerlines;
>   (2) oil pipelines, including pipelines connecting the onshore storage facilities

of a deepwater port . . . , gas pipelines, sulphur pipelines, and other electric lines and pipelines of any nature;

(3) irrigation canals, laterals, and water pipelines;

(4) roads; and

(5) any other purpose the commissioner considers to be in the best interest of the state.

(b) Consent to conduct an activity that would disturb or remove marl, sand, gravel, shell, or mudshell on or near the surface of a state-owned riverbed or the bed of a navigable stream in the public domain may be granted only under Chapter 86, Parks and Wildlife Code.

(c) Money received by the land office for the grants of easements through and under the state-owned riverbeds and beds of navigable streams in the public domain shall be deposited in a special fund account in the state treasury to be used for the removal or improvement of unauthorized structures on permanent school fund land. This fund does not impose a duty or obligation on the state to accept ownership of, remove, or improve unauthorized structures on permanent school fund land.

Natural Resources Code § 51.302. Prohibition and Penalty:

(a) No person may construct or maintain any structure or facility on land owned by the state, nor may any person who has not acquired a proper easement, lease, permit, or other instrument from the state as required by this chapter or Chapter 33 of this code and who owns or possesses a facility or structure that is now located on or across state land continue in possession of the land unless he obtains from the commissioner, the board, or the board of regents an easement, lease, permit, or other instrument required by this chapter or Chapter 33 of this code for the land on which the facility or structure is to be constructed or is located.

(b) A person who constructs, maintains, owns, or possesses a facility or structure on state land without a proper easement or lease from the state under this chapter or under Chapter 33 of this code is liable for a penalty of not less than $50 or more than $1,000 a day for each day that a violation occurs. The penalty shall be recovered by the commissioner under Section 51.3021 of this code or in a civil action by the attorney general.

(c) A person who owns, maintains, or possesses an unauthorized facility or structure is, for purposes of this section, the person who last owned, maintained, or possessed the facility or structure.

(d) The commissioner or attorney general may also recover from a person who constructs, maintains, owns, or possesses a facility or structure on state land without the proper easement the costs to the state of removing that facility or structure under Section 51.3021 of this code.

(e) Penalties and costs recovered under this section shall be deposited in the special fund established under Sections 52.297 and 53.155 of this code.

(f) This section is cumulative of all other applicable penalties or enforcement provisions of this code.

(g) In lieu of seeking administrative penalties or removal of the facility or structure under Section 51.3021 of this code, the commissioner may elect to accept ownership of the facility or structure as a fixture and may exercise the state's rights as owner of the facility or structure by filing notice of such ownership in the real property records of the county in which the facility or structure is located. For facilities or structures located on coastal public land, notice of ownership shall be filed in the county adjacent to the property on which the facility or structure is located. A notice under this subsection shall contain a legal description of the adjacent property, the owner of property if known, and a description of the facility or structure. A state agency fund or trust fund is not liable for the condition of any facility or structure as a result of acquiring an interest in the facility or structure under this section.

Natural Resources Code § 51.3021. Removal of Facility or Structure by Commissioner:

(a) The commissioner may remove and dispose of a facility or structure on land owned by the state if the commissioner finds the facility or structure to be:
    (1) without the proper easement or lease from the state under Chapter 33 or 51 of this code; or
    (2) an imminent and unreasonable threat to public health, safety, or welfare.
(b)–(g) [procedures for removal].

Authority of Governor

Natural Resources Code § 11.076(a):

If the governor is credibly informed that any portion of the public land or the land which belongs to any of the special funds has been enclosed or that fences have been erected on the land in violation of law, he may direct the attorney general to institute suit in the name of the state for the recovery of the land, damages, and fees.

Authority of Attorney General

Natural Resources Code §11.077. Suit against Adverse Claimant:

If any public land is held, occupied, or claimed adversely to the state or to any fund of the state by any person or if land is forfeited to the state for any reason, the attorney general shall file suit for the land, for rent on the land, and to recover damages to the land.

Permit for Disturbing or Taking of Marl, Sand, Gravel, etc.

Parks and Wildlife Code § 86.001. Management and Protection:

> The [Parks and Wildlife] commission shall manage, control, and protect marl and sand of commercial value and all gravel, shell, and mudshell located within the tidewater limits of the state, and on islands within those limits, and within the freshwater areas of the state not embraced by a survey of private land, and on islands within those areas.

Parks and Wildlife Code § 86.002:

> (a) No person may disturb or take marl, sand, gravel, shell, or mudshell under the management and protection of the commission or operate in or disturb any oyster bed or fishing water for any purpose other than that necessary or incidental to navigation or dredging under state or federal authority without first having acquired from the commission a permit authorizing the activity.

Permitting of Bridges

Trice v. *State*, 712 S.W.2d 842 (Tex.App.—Waco 1986, writ ref'd n.r.e.) discussed who was allowed to bridge Texas streams under the laws then in effect. The court noted (at p. 847):

> The State, through legislative action, has also authorized certain entities to erect bridges over the navigable waters within its boundaries [citing statutes pertaining to counties, municipalities, railroads, and toll road corporations]. However, except for its tidal waters, the State has not authorized an individual to construct a bridge over its navigable waters. Furthermore, the State has not created an agency or designated any public official to regulate bridge construction over its navigable waters.

Under a change in law in 1993, the Commissioner of the General Land Office was granted limited permitting power to allow private road crossings over public streams. See Natural Resources Code § 51.291 (quoted on pp. 184–85).

Permitting of Dams by the Texas Natural Resource Conservation Commission

Water Code § 11.121. Permit Required:

> Except as provided in Sections 11.142, 11.1421, and 11.1422 of this code, no person may appropriate any state water or begin construction of any work

designed for the storage, taking, or diversion of water without first obtaining a permit from the commission to make the appropriation.

Water Code § 11.142. Permit Exemptions:

(a) Without obtaining a permit, a person may construct on his own property a dam or reservoir to impound or contain not more than 200 acre-feet of water for domestic and livestock purposes.

(b) Without obtaining a permit, a person who is drilling and producing petroleum and conducting operations associated with drilling and producing petroleum may take for those purposes state water from the Gulf of Mexico and adjacent bays and arms of the Gulf of Mexico in an amount not to exceed one acre-foot during each 24-hour period.

(c) Without obtaining a permit, a person may construct or maintain a reservoir for the sole purpose of sediment control as part of a surface coal mining operation under the Texas Surface Coal Mining and Reclamation Act (Article 5920-11, Vernon's Texas Civil Statutes).

Water Code § 11.1421. Permit Exemption for Mariculture Activities [Using Brackish or Marine Water].

Water Code § 11.1422. Permit Exemption for Historic Cemeteries.

Ownership of Beds of Navigable Streams

The beds of navigable streams are generally owned by the state, in trust for the public. Most of the land alongside navigable streams is privately owned. The beds of non-navigable streams are usually privately owned, and public use of the stream may be forbidden by the private landowner. However, the state owns the beds of perennial streams, regardless of navigability, where the original land grant was made under the civil law prior to December 14, 1837.

Under a 1929 law popularly known as the "Small Bill," the state in some situations has relinquished to the adjoining landowner certain property rights in the bed of a navigable stream. However, the public may still use these navigable streams. The law's major effect was to give some adjoining landowners the royalties from oil and gas under the streambed. Significantly, the Small Bill declared that it did not impair the rights of the general public and the state in the waters of streams. Thus, along a navigable stream, even if the landowner's deed includes the bed, and taxes are being paid on the bed, the public retains its right to use it as a navigable stream. The Small Bill also retained the state's sand and gravel interests.

≈ ≈ ≈ ≈ ≈

State Ownership in Trust for the Public

> [O]ur decisions are unanimous in the declaration that by the principles of the civil and common law soil under navigable waters was treated as held by the state or nation in trust for the whole people. *State* v. *Bradford*, 121 Tex. 515, 50 S.W.2d 1065, 1076 (1932).

> The waters of public navigable streams are held by the State in trust for the public, primarily for navigation purposes. *Carrithers* v. *Terramar Beach Com. Imp. Ass'n*, 645 S.W.2d 772, 774 (Tex. 1983).

> [T]itle to [a navigable stream's] waters is in the state in trust for the public. . . . The waters are in trust for the public: First, for navigation purposes, which concerns all the public and is ordinarily regarded as a superior right. *Motl* v. *Boyd*, 116 Tex. 82, 286 S.W. 458, 468 (1926).

State Ownership of Perennial Streams under the Civil Law

Manry v. *Robison*, 122 Tex. 213, 231; 56 S.W. 2d 438, 446 (1932) states:

> The status of the law in Texas when we adopted the common law as the rule of decision in 1840 was as follows: Texas owned the beds of all *perennial streams, regardless of navigability*, whether grants of land adjacent were made by Spain and Mexico prior to March 2, 1836, or by the Republic of Texas prior to the Act of [December 14,] 1837, *by virtue of the civil law of Mexico.* . . . The Republic also owned the beds of all streams touching grants made subsequent to that date and prior to the Act of 1840, *whether perennial or not*, where the beds were as wide as 30 feet, under the Mexican civil law as modified by the Act of 1837.

For an example of a stream found to be perennial, see *Heard* v. *Town of Refugio*, 103 S.W.2d 728, 729–30 (Tex. 1937).

The Small Bill

The Small Bill is codified as Article 5414a of the Revised Civil Statutes of Texas. It allows, under certain circumstances, a landowner with insufficient upland acreage in a land grant to make up the difference by claiming acreage from the streambed.

One provision of the Small Bill states:

> [N]othing in this Act contained shall impair the rights of the general public and the State in the waters of streams.

In a 1932 case addressing the nature of the private ownership granted by the Small Bill, the Texas Supreme Court noted:

The reservation to the state and the public of the waters of streams would, under well-established rules of construction, carry with the reservation all things necessary to the practicable and substantial use of and enjoyment of the things reserved. *State v. Bradford*, 121 Tex. 515, 50 S.W. 2d 1065, 1077 (1932).

Dams and the Small Bill

See *Garrison v. Bexar-Medina-Atascosa Counties W. I. D.*, 404 S.W. 2d 376 (Tex. Civ.App.—Austin 1966), holding approved and writ ref'd, n.r.e., 407 S.W. 2d 771 (Tex. 1966). The headnotes to the opinions summarize the case as follows:

> The Small Bill which confirmed patents and awards to beds of water courses and navigable streams did not vest patentees and their assignees with such title as would constitute beds of navigable streams their "own property" within meaning of statute permitting construction of dam or reservoir on their own property without a permit.

> Statute permitting landowners to construct dam on their own property without permit has no application to a stream which is navigable as defined by statute relating to navigable streams which shall not be crossed by the lines on a survey.

See Water Code § 11.142 (formerly in Art. 7500a) and Natural Resources Code § 21.001 (formerly in Art. 5302).

Navigation Rights Irrespective of Ownership

A lawsuit was brought by some landowners who claimed ownership of the bed of the Upper Guadalupe. They contended that their titles were impaired when the Texas Water Rights Commission found (and the trial court affirmed) that the stream is navigable by statute. The appeals court rejected the landowners' contention, stating:

> The title of owners of beds of streams by the State or landowners does not determine property rights in the water. Assuming that the property owners here involved owned the stream beds, this does not deprive the State from reasonable regulations and control of navigable streams. A property owner, including holders of riparian rights, cannot unreasonably impair the public's rights of navigation and access to and enjoyment of a navigable water course. *Adjudication of Upper Guadalupe Segment of Guadalupe River Basin*, 625 S.W.2d 353, 362 (Tex.Civ. App.—San Antonio 1981), *aff'd*, 642 S.W. 2d 438 (1982).

The Gradient Boundary

Texas courts have adopted the "gradient boundary" as the usual dividing line between public ownership of a stream's bed and lower bank area, and private ownership of the higher bank area and the uplands beyond. Thus, there is generally no question as to the public's right to use the bank area up to the gradient boundary. Sometimes called the "mean" gradient boundary, it is located midway between the lower level of the flowing water that just reaches the so-called "cut bank," and the higher level of the flowing water that just does not overtop the cut bank. The cut bank is located at the outer edge of a stream's bed, separating the bed from the adjacent upland and confining the waters to a definite channel. Surveying the gradient boundary is a complex task performable only by specially trained persons.

Judicial Description of the Gradient Boundary

The gradient boundary concept was developed in a U.S. Supreme Court case involving the boundary between Oklahoma and Texas along the south bank of the Red River. After considering the terms of an 1819 treaty between the United States and Spain, the Supreme Court concluded:

> Upon the authority of these cases, and upon principle as well, we hold that the bank intended by the treaty provision is the water-washed and relatively permanent elevation or acclivity at the outer line of the river bed which separates the bed from the adjacent upland, whether valley or hill, and serves to confine the waters within the bed and to preserve the course of the river, and that the boundary intended is on and along the bank at the average or mean level attained by the waters in the periods when they reach and wash the bank without overflowing it. When we speak of the bed we include all of the area which is kept practically bare of vegetation by the wash of the waters of the river from year to year in their onward course, although parts of it are left dry for months at a time; and we exclude the lateral valleys, which have the characteristics of relatively fast land and usually are covered by upland grasses and vegetation, although temporarily overflowed in exceptional instances when the river is at flood.

> The conclusion that the boundary intended is on and along the bank and not at low-water mark or any other point within the river bed has full confirmation in available historical data respecting the negotiations which attended the framing and signing of the treaty. *Oklahoma* v. *Texas*, 260 U.S. 606, 631–32, 43 S.Ct. 221, 225, 67 L. Ed. 428 (1923).

In *Motl* v. *Boyd*, 116 Tex. 82, 286 S.W. 458, 467 (1926), the Texas Supreme Court used language much like that used by the U.S. Supreme Court to describe the bed and the bank of a stream:

> A water course, river, or stream consists of a bed, banks, and a stream of water. . . . The bed of a stream is that portion of its soil which is alternatively covered and left bare as there may be an increase or diminution in the supply of water, and which is adequate to contain it at its average and mean stage during an entire year, without reference to the extra freshets of the winter or spring or the extreme drouths of the summer or autumn. . . . The banks of a stream or river are the water-washed and relatively permanent elevations or acclivities at the outer lines of the river bed which separate the bed from the adjacent upland, whether valley

or hill, and served to confine the waters within the bed and preserve the course of the river when they rise to the highest point at which they are still confined to a definite channel.

In a 1935 case, the Texas Supreme Court endorsed the gradient boundary concept, stating:

The boundary line is a gradient of the flowing water in the river. It is located midway between the lower level of the flowing water that just reaches the cut bank, and the higher level of it that just does not overtop the cut bank. *Diversion Lake Club* v. *Heath*, 126 Tex. 129, 86 S.W. 2d 441, 447 (1935).

Criminal Trespass

As part of the navigation right, one may use the bed and, to a limited degree, the banks of a navigable stream. However, the use of the private property adjacent to a stream can be a criminal trespass.

Under Texas Penal Code § 30.05 (see below), the definition of criminal trespass is more complex than the simple notion of being on someone else's land. One way to commit the offense is to enter upon another's property even though one has notice that the entry is forbidden. Another way is to remain on another's property, refusing to leave after receiving notice to depart.

Notice can be given in any one of five forms. First, it can be an oral or written communication by the owner or someone acting for the owner. Second, it can be a fence or other enclosure obviously designed to exclude intruders or to contain live-stock. Third, notice can be in the form of sign(s) posted on the property or at the en-trance to the building, reasonably likely to be noticed, indicating that entry is forbid-den. Fourth, notice can be in the form of readily visible purple paint marks of proper size and placement on trees or posts spaced no more than 100 feet apart on forest land and 1,000 feet apart on nonforest land. Fifth, notice can be the visible presence on the property of a crop grown for human consumption that is under cultivation, in the pro-cess of being harvested, or marketable if harvested at the time of entry.

Criminal trespass is normally a Class B misdemeanor with a fine up to $2,000 and a jail term up to 180 days. Under certain conditions—including if one has a deadly weapon on or about one's person—the offense is a Class A misdemeanor with a fine up to $4,000 and a jail term up to one year.

≈ ≈ ≈ ≈ ≈

Penal Code § 30.05. Criminal Trespass:

(a) A person commits an offense if he enters or remains on property or in a build-ing of another without effective consent and he
  (1) had notice that the entry was forbidden; or
  (2) received notice to depart but failed to do so.
(b) For purposes of this section,
  (1) "Entry" means the intrusion of the entire body.

(2) "Notice" means:

   (A) oral or written communication by the owner or someone with apparent authority to act for the owner;

   (B) fencing or other enclosure obviously designed to exclude intruders or to contain livestock; or

   (C) a sign or signs posted on the property or at the entrance to the building, reasonably likely to come to the attention of intruders, indicating that entry is forbidden;

   (D) the placement of identifying purple paint marks on trees or posts on the property, provided that the marks are

      (i) vertical lines of not less than eight inches in length and not less than one inch in width;

      (ii) placed so that the bottom of the mark is not less than three feet from the ground or more than five feet from the ground; and

      (iii) placed at locations that are readily visible to any person approaching the property and no more than:

         (a) 100 feet apart on forest land; or

         (b) 1,000 feet apart on land other than forest land; or

   (E) the visible presence on the property of a crop grown for human consumption that is under cultivation, in the process of being harvested, or marketable if harvested at the time of entry.

(3) "Shelter center" has the meaning assigned by Section 51.002(1), Human Resources Code.

(4) "Forest land" means land on which the trees are potentially valuable for timber products.

(c) It is a defense to prosecution under this section that the actor at the time of the offense was a fire fighter or emergency medical services personnel, as that term is defined by Section 773.003, Health and Safety Code, acting in the lawful discharge of an official duty under exigent circumstances.

(d) An offense under this section is a Class B misdemeanor unless it is committed in a habitation or a shelter center or unless the actor carries a deadly weapon on or about his person during the commission of the offense, in which event it is a Class A misdemeanor.

Use of Stream Bank to Scout and Portage Hazards

Historically, the law of Texas, both in statute and in common law, has protected public rights relating to navigable streams. Although there appears to be no Texas statute or case specifically dealing with scouting or portaging, several aspects of Texas law seem to support the proposition that a portage right is a necessary corollary to the fundamental right of navigation. The authorities set out below support the principle that when a person floating a navigable stream encounters an obstruction like a log jam or a dam, or some other potential safety hazard, the navigator has a limited privilege to go onto adjoining private land to scout and if necessary make a safe, reasonable portage. The intrusion on private land should be minimized. Other states that have addressed the issue concur in recognizing a portage right. Of course, as is sometimes the case, particular or peculiar fact situations may alter the application of general concepts in specific instances.

There is a fundamental distinction between using private land to portage around an obstacle and using private land as a short cut to get to or from a river. In Texas one has no right in general to cut through private land simply for convenient access to or from a stream.

≈ ≈ ≈ ≈ ≈

Portaging Obstructions as a Traditional Part of Navigation

Obstructions have always been a natural part of streams. As the waters flow through the land, streams become obstructed by fallen trees, log jams, rapids, sand bars, shoals, etc. Historical accounts of navigating streams often mention the hazards and portages encountered. See, for example, Kenneth G. Roberts and Philip Shackleton, *The Canoe: A History of the Craft from Panama to the Arctic* (1983). Thus, portaging has always been a part of navigation.

The U.S. Supreme Court has explained that under the federal test of navigability (involving capacity for use in interstate commerce) the presence of a portage does not defeat navigability:

> Navigability, in the sense of the law, is not destroyed because the water course is interrupted by occasional natural obstructions or portages; nor need the navigation be open at all seasons of the year, or at all stages of the water. *Economy Light & Power Co.* v. *United States*, 256 U.S. 113, 122, 41 S.Ct. 409, 412 (1921).

As discussed above, Texas law has long recognized the public's navigation right, a right of free passage along navigable streams. As set out above, Texas law disfavors obstructions to navigation. The right to navigate would be meaningless if the presence of a single hazard—a fallen tree, for example—could legally "cut off" navigability.

Advice to Scout and Portage Contained in National Publications

The American Red Cross, *Canoeing and Kayaking* (1981), pp. 5.12–5.15.
Dave Harrison, *Sports Illustrated Canoeing* (1981), pp. 154–55.
William "Bill" Hillcourt, *Official Boy Scout Handbook* (1979), p. 161.

Advice to Scout and Portage Containce in Local Publications

Texas Rivers and Rapids, a commercial guide describing commonly used waterways, has been through several editions over the past two decades. It advises a number of portages on various streams. Volume 2, published in 1973, includes this advice in a discussion of river currents: "Never run a dam or drop unless absolutely necessary." The book cautions, for example, of a portage along the Clear Fork of the Trinity River near Fort Worth:

Roll's Dam is approximately ten feet high and should not be run. It is an easy portage on the right bank adjacent to the dam at low water levels. At high levels, the portage is longer and must be started on the left bank quite a way upstream from the dam. Use the left bank portage only when necessary because you will have to travel on private property behind a house.

Volume 6 of *Texas Rivers and Rapids*, published in 1983, warns of particular hazards potentially requiring portage on a number of rivers, including the Brazos, the Colorado, the Frio, the Guadalupe, the Leon, the Neches, the Pecos, the Rio Grande, the San Marcos, and the Trinity. It also cautions of log jams on several streams.

The Big Bend Natural History Association in cooperation with the National Park Service publishes guides to floating the Rio Grande, not only within Big Bend National Park but also downstream along the Lower Canyons. The Lower Canyons guide advises boaters of several locations where challenging rapids should be scouted or portaged, including using private land along the Texas side of the river.

The Lower Colorado River Authority has published a guide to the Lower Colorado River, from Austin to the Gulf of Mexico. In its discussion of public and private river rights, the guide contains the following passage (p. 13):

Along the Colorado River, almost all the land outside of the riverbed is privately owned. However, if a boater encounters a hazard like a log jam, low-water dam or some other obstruction, the boater may get out and scout to see whether there is a safe route through and portage if boating would be dangerous. The intrusion on private land should at all times be minimized.

The Greater New Braunfels Chamber of Commerce distributes the "Guadalupe River Scenic Area Information Map and Pamphlet." It highlights the time-honored advice, "When in doubt stop and scout." The map of the Lower Guadalupe marks the locations of dangerous falls, rapids, and dams, as well as the low bridge at Gruene. It also states, "Do not run Horseshoe Falls."

The City of New Braunfels has posted maps of the popular Comal River at several public access points. Those maps note two spots where "Safe By-Pass Steps" are available to allow passage around rapids. One spot is just above the tube chute, and the other is just above the old Camp Warnecke dam (now adjacent to the Schlitterbahn water park).

Use of Stream Banks under Civil Law

The civil law (the law of Spain and Mexico, and the early days of the Republic of Texas) recognized the right of a navigator to use the banks, even though privately owned, for various purposes associated with navigation. The civil law still applies to particular land grants. The permitted activities set out in law 6 of title 28 of the third *Partida* (quoted below) amount to what might be considered today as fairly substantial uses. It is difficult to imagine that a generally less intrusive use involved in a portage would be forbidden.

Law 6. *That Every One may Make Use of Ports, Rivers, and Public Roads.*— Rivers, ports, and public roads belong to all men in common; so that strangers coming from foreign countries may make use of them, in the same manner as the inhabitants of the place where they are. And though the dominion or property (*señorío*) of the banks of rivers belongs to the owner of the adjoining estate, nevertheless, every man may make use of them to fasten his vessel to the trees that grow there, or to refit his vessel, or to put his sails or merchandise there. So fishermen may put and expose their fish for sale there, and dry their nets, or make use of the banks for all like purposes, which appertain to the art or trade by which they live.

The Common Law

Since January 20, 1840, the common law has been included as part of the rule of decision for Texas courts. The pertinent statute now reads:

> The rule of decision in this state consists of those portions of the common law of England that are not inconsistent with the constitution or the laws of this state, the constitution of this state, and the laws of this state. Texas Civil Practice and Remedies Code § 5.001.

As explained by the Texas Supreme Court, this statute is not an adoption of the common law as it was in force in England in 1840, but rather of the common law as declared by the courts of the different states of the United States. See *Grigsby* v. *Reib*, 153 S.W. 1124, 1125 (Tex. 1913).

Recognition by Other States

A right to portage has been explicitly recognized in a number of states in a variety of contexts. For example:

Montana. The Supreme Court of Montana in construing Montana law has stated:

> Therefore, we hold that the public has a right to use state-owned waters to the point of the high-water mark except to the extent of barriers in the waters. In the case of barriers, the public is allowed to portage around such barriers in the least intrusive way possible, avoiding damage to the private property holder's rights. . . . [T]he right to portage must be accomplished in the least intrusive manner possible. *Montana Coalition for Stream Access* v. *Curran*, 682 P.2d 163, 172 (Mont. 1984).

Ohio. The Ohio Attorney General has concluded:

> The reasonably necessary entry of a boater upon land adjacent to a dam obstructing a navigable watercourse in order to portage his boat around the dam by the nearest practical route and in a reasonable manner constitutes a privileged

intrusion on the property of the landowner. Op. Ohio Att'y Gen. No. 80-094 (1980).

Nebraska. A Nebraska statute allows an affirmative defense to a criminal trespass charge if:

> The actor was in the process of navigating or attempting to navigate with a non-powered vessel any stream or river in this state and found it necessary to portage or otherwise transport the vessel around any fence or obstructions in such stream or river. Neb. Rev. Stat. § 28-522.

New York. Under New York law, the beds of most navigable streams are privately held, subject to the public's rights. A recent court opinion rejected a plaintiff landowner's attempt to obtain a summary judgment for trespass against boaters who had scouted and portaged in a navigable stream's bed:

> Pursuant to the public trust doctrine, the public right of navigation in navigable waters supersedes plaintiff's private right in the land under the water. . . . Plaintiff contends that the public right of navigation is limited to riding in boats and does not include the right to get out of a canoe and walk in the bed of the river to guide the canoe through shallow water, avoid rocks or portage around rapids. According to plaintiff, the absence of any case law specifically including such activities in the public right of navigation establishes that no such right exists. Defendants contend that the public right of navigation includes the right to engage in reasonable activities that are incidental to and necessary for navigating the river. The absence of case law, according to defendants, is the result of no one ever having previously claimed that the public right of navigation did not include the use of the river bed to portage or engage in other activities incidental to and necessary for navigation. We agree with defendants. *Adirondack League Club Inc.* v. *Sierra Club*, 615 N.Y.S.2d 788, 792 (A.D. 3 Dept. 1994), *appeal dismissed* 622 N.Y.S.2d 917.

Texts Summarizing the Common Law

Legal texts summarizing the common law typically contain statements of legal principles supporting portaging. For example, the American Law Institute has recognized a limited privilege by a navigator to enter the otherwise private land next to a river:

> The privilege of navigation carries with it the ancillary privilege to enter on riparian land to the extent that this is necessary for the accomplishment of the purpose of the principal privilege. *Restatement (Second) of Torts* § 193, Comment d (1965).

The portage right is a specific application of this privilege. Of course, a navigator's right does not extend to a general sort of wandering or sightseeing upon a pasture near the river, because such wandering or sightseeing on private land is not necessary to carry out the navigation right.

A Riparian or Dam Builder's Permit Does Not Preclude Navigation

A Texas case has explained that the state's grant of permission to dam a navigable stream does not include permission to preclude navigation:

> It gave no title to the water, but only the right to divert and use so much of the water appropriated as might be necessarily required when beneficially used for the purpose for which it was appropriated. . . . It gave no title to the fish in the water of the lake, no exclusive right to take the fish from the lake, and no right to interfere with the public in their use of the river and its water for navigation, fishing, and other lawful purposes further than interference necessarily result-[ing] from the construction and maintenance of the dams and lakes in such manner as reasonably to accomplish the purpose of the appropriation. *Diversion Lake Club* v. *Heath*, 126 Tex. 129, 86 S.W. 2d 441, 446 (1935).

As to private impairment of navigation, a recent Texas case stated:

> The title of owners of beds of streams by the State or landowners does not determine property rights in the water. Assuming that the property owners here involved owned the stream beds, this does not deprive the State from reasonable regulations and control of navigable streams. A property owner, including holders of riparian rights, cannot unreasonably impair the public's rights of navigation and access to and enjoyment of a navigable water course. *Adjudication of Upper Guadalupe Segment of Guadalupe River Basin*, 625 S.W. 2d 353, 362 (Tex.Civ.App.—San Antonio 1981), *aff'd*, 642 S.W.2d 438 (1982).

The Criminal Law

There seems to be no reported case in Texas involving a prosecution for trespass for a navigator's portage. The "necessity defense" could be asserted by a navigator charged with criminal trespass during a portage. Texas Penal Code § 9.22 (see below) allows conduct that would otherwise be a crime to be considered justified if three conditions are met. Note that this defense requires a weighing of harms. Assuming there is no special harm to the private property, going onto private land for a reasonable portage would fall within this defense.

Penal Code § 9.22. Necessity:

> Conduct is justified if
> (1) the actor reasonably believes the conduct is immediately necessary to avoid imminent harm;
> (2) the desirability and urgency of avoiding the harm clearly outweigh, according

to ordinary standards of reasonableness, the harm sought to be prevented by the law prescribing the conduct; and

(3) a legislative purpose to exclude the justification claimed for the conduct does not otherwise plainly appear.

Penal Code § 1.07(a)(25):

"Harm" means anything reasonably regarded as loss, disadvantage, or injury, including harm to another person in whose welfare the person affected is interested.

Consideration of the Navigation Right as an Easement

In various jurisdictions the navigation right has sometimes been compared to or referred to as an easement. A Texas legal text has stated the following about easements in general:

Every easement carries with it the right to do such things as are reasonably necessary for the full enjoyment of the easement, and the extent to which incidental rights may be exercised depends on the object and purpose of the grant and whether such rights are limited by its terms. But the exercise of the right must be such as will not injuriously increase the burden on the servient owner, and there may be no use that will interfere with the servient owner's free enjoyment of that part of his property not affected by the easement. The owner of an easement and the possessor of the servient estate are to exercise their respective rights and privileges in a spirit of mutual accommodation. 31 Tex.Jur. 3d *Easements & Licenses in Real Property* § 43 (1984).

Common Law as the Perfection of Reason

It has been asserted that the common law is "the perfection of reason." See *Welder* v. *State*, 196 S.W. 868, 870 (Tex.Civ.App.—Austin 1917, writ ref'd). In light of the fundamental right of public navigation, it is not reasonable to expect a navigator to risk life, limb, or property by attempting to navigate through a hazard. Past and present Texans have used their common sense to scout and, if necessary, portage obstructions along Texas rivers.

Index